GUIDEBOOK
FOR SMALL GROUP & INDIVIDUAL STUDY

GODQUEST

*Discover the God
Your Heart Is Searching For*

SEAN McDOWELL   JENNIFER DION

OUTRE/CH®

***GodQuest* Guidebook**
Copyright © 2011 by Sean McDowell

Outreach, Inc., Vista CA 92081
Outreach.com

All Scripture quotations, unless otherwise indicated, are taken from the HOLY BIBLE, NEW INTERNATIONAL VERSION®. Copyright © 1973, 1978, 1984 Biblica. Used by permission of Zondervan. All rights reserved.

Scripture quotations marked (NLT) are taken from the *Holy Bible,* New Living Translation, copyright © 1996, 2004, 2007 by Tyndale House Foundation. Used by permission of Tyndale House Publishers, Inc., Carol Stream, Illinois 60188. All rights reserved.

Scripture quotations marked (NASB) are taken from the NEW AMERICAN STANDARD BIBLE®, Copyright © 1960, 1962, 1963, 1968, 1971, 1972, 1973, 1975, 1977, 1995 by The Lockman Foundation. Used by permission.

ISBN: 978-1-9355-4133-2

Cover and interior design: Tim Downs and Alexia Wuerdeman
Editing: Toni Ridgaway and Diane Stortz
GodQuest video design and production: 4120Productions.com

Printed in the United States of America

CONTENTS

INTRODUCTION

My steps have held to your paths; my feet have not slipped. —Psalm 17:5

I (Jennifer) think my mom and dad secretly dread traveling with me. My parents' trips are carefully researched, well planned, and meticulously recorded with dates, times, and phone numbers on a handwritten itinerary. In contrast, when I fly somewhere, I usually skid up to the boarding gate with my luggage flipped over my shoulder, a computer-printed boarding pass in one hand, and a hot café mocha spilling onto my other hand. Before my parents leave on a trip, they stop at the travel club to pick up maps and information on area attractions, restaurants, and hotels. I visit an online map site the night before I leave, print a page or two of directions, and then toss them on the passenger seat of my car. My parents have learned that careful planning and communication help avoid wrong turns and disappointment. I long ago decided that speed and convenience are what matter, and almost any travel disaster can be solved with a credit card and a cell phone.

A few years ago, however, my casual travel habits finally caught up with me. My parents had invited us to join them for a family reunion in beautiful Cape Hatteras. The Outer Banks of North Carolina were the site of my best childhood vacation, and the memories of bobbing in the Atlantic and digging for elusive sand crabs drew me on as we departed Williamsburg, Virginia, on an early evening drive down to Cape Hatteras.

In my usual fashion, I had gotten directions online and had them tucked in the car as my kids and I began the drive south to North Carolina. As we swung east around Norfolk, I read from the directions:

Merge onto VA-168 S via EXIT 291B (crossing into North Carolina). 16.2 Miles.

From there, the directions indicated that VA-168 turned into NC-168 and continued for another 18.3 miles. As the better part of an hour passed and the night grew darker, I slowly realized that we had driven for way more than 16.2 plus 18.3 miles. Cold adrenaline trickled down my spine, and I desperately wondered, *What happened?* I drove on for another ten or so miles and then mentally conceded we were lost, without a map, and obviously not on the NC-168 headed for the Outer Banks. I pulled into a remote, poorly lit gas station, told the kids to stay in the car, and cautiously approached a man standing by one of the pumps. Yes, he answered, I was still in North Carolina, but no, I was not even close to the Outer Banks. I had somehow taken the wrong exit and driven over an hour in the wrong direction!

GODQUEST

It was a long, frustrating experience. At the end of the night, though, I had driven an hour back to the right exit and then correctly followed the directions another ninety minutes southeast to Cape Hatteras. So it was not a fun trip, but in the end, taking the wrong road only cost me two hours of wasted time.

Taking the wrong "road" in life, however, can be much more costly. The Bible says this:

> "Enter through the narrow gate. For wide is the gate and broad is the road that leads to destruction, and many enter through it. But small is the gate and narrow the road that leads to life, and only a few find it."
> —Matthew 7:13–14

This passage teaches an important truth: the daily choices we make and the paths we choose at the big forks in the road of life have a tremendous impact on our present lives—and on our ultimate destinations. In his book *The Screwtape Letters*, British author C. S. Lewis noted, "The safest road to Hell is the gradual one—the gentle slope, soft underfoot, without sudden turnings, without milestones, without Signposts." According to Lewis, hell is not just a destination some people go to in the afterlife, it is the culmination of a lifelong journey.

Knowing what to believe and where to go in life can be confusing, even intimidating. In the face of a dizzying array of spiritual choices, how can we decide which path to take? For the next six weeks, we are going on a quest—an adventurous journey to discover the source of the universe and the meaning of life. Along the way, we will encounter six Signposts that will help you consider what you believe about the Bible, creation and the existence of God, who Jesus was, the problem of pain and suffering, and which path or paths lead to Heaven. These six Signposts are reliable, biblical, unchanging, and designed to help you arrive at your life's destination.

If you don't already know God, these Signposts will help you find Him and experience a relationship that will change your life. If you already have a relationship with God, these Signposts will draw you closer to Him and help keep you on the right path in life. The *GodQuest* is not about finding truth and then moving on with your life. It's about knowing the Creator of the universe and discovering His plan for you.

As you journey, we believe you will discover a God who is true to this promise: *Trust in the LORD with all your heart and lean not on your own understanding; in all your ways acknowledge him, and he will make your paths straight* (Proverbs 3:5–6).

Using Your Guidebook

He guides me in paths of righteousness for his name's sake. —Psalm 23:3

Recently, I (Sean) took a group of students on a tour of Israel and Turkey. The guidebook we consulted helped ensure the success of our trip, thanks to its collection of maps, interesting facts, and historical background for each of the sites we visited. Similarly, this Guidebook will provide you with all the directions and information you need for your six-week *GodQuest*. The Guidebook includes instructions for group study, travel tips to help you get the most from *GodQuest*, map legends full of background information, thought-provoking discussion questions, and five daily *Travel Logs* to help you consider new information and record your thoughts.

Use your Guidebook in conjunction with the *GodQuest* DVD-based Study. If you're doing the study in a small group, one person in the group will need to have the *GodQuest* DVD-based Study kit, which includes a *GodQuest* Guidebook, a Leader's Guide, and a DVD with six video lessons. You can also do the *GodQuest* study on your own, with your spouse or friends, or with the other members of your family. You will need to have one *GodQuest* DVD-based Study kit for your group and a *GodQuest* Guidebook for each person participating in the study.

Format for GodQuest Weekly Studies

Each *GodQuest* weekly study includes a video lesson with associated questions, *The Weekly Quest* (suggestions for further investigation of the topics that interest you), and five short daily studies called *Travel Logs*. Each week, follow the lesson in the order presented in this Guidebook. The chart on the next page has a description of each *GodQuest* weekly lesson, along with recommendations on how to spread the lesson out over the week.

GODQUEST

SECTION	DESCRIPTION	TIMING & RECOMMENDATIONS
Weekly video lesson and study questions	Ten- to twelve-minute video lesson. Eight to eleven study questions, including: • Icebreaker question • Several questions regarding the video lesson • Bible verses and application questions	You will want to choose a day of the week for watching the video lesson and completing the group study (you can do the study on your own, with your family, or with a few friends if you aren't involved in a small group).
The Weekly Quest	This section of your Guidebook will have suggestions about websites you can visit, topics you can research, and books, videos, or movies that will challenge your thinking and help you build your faith.	Read *The Weekly Quest* the day after you watch the video lesson and complete the study questions. You can visit the websites, read books, or review the suggested material at any time.
Travel Logs	There are five daily *Travel Logs* with a mix of facts, questions, short biographies, and activities. Each *Travel Log* is two pages in length.	Do one *Travel Log* each day after you have completed the video lesson and questions and have read *The Weekly Quest*.

Below is a description of each section in *GodQuest* weekly studies.

Prayer

We recommend that you open and close each lesson with prayer.

Starting Location

Before beginning any journey, you need to know your starting location. Use these first questions to determine where you are in your views.

Directions from Your Guides

Watch the *GodQuest* video lesson for the week; then use the associated questions to review the lesson and discuss the main points made by your *GodQuest* video guides (Sean McDowell and eight guests).

Trip Planner

This section includes a number of Bible passages that deal with the week's topic, along with discussion questions for each Scripture.

The Weekly Quest

This section is described in the previous table.

Travel Logs

The *Travel Logs* have interesting facts, questions, activities, and short biographies. The last *Travel Log* for the week is *Reflections from Your Journey*. In this final *Travel Log*, you will spend some time thinking about what you've learned and then reflect on your own spiritual search.

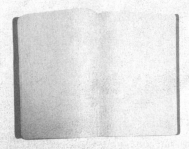

GODQUEST

SMALL GROUP GUIDELINES (if you are doing the *GodQuest* study in a small group or Sunday school class)

Small groups can have an enormous impact on your life and faith. They help you build friendships and provide support, and they offer you a close group of people who can encourage you and hold you accountable. These guidelines will help you get the most from your time together:

CONFIDENTIALITY: Everything shared in your group should be considered confidential unless you are given specific permission to share it elsewhere. Confidentiality protects your group and allows it to be a supportive, accepting place for everyone.

OPENNESS: Do your best to be open and honest during discussions. Your transparency will encourage others to do the same.

RESPECT: Everyone has the right to his or her opinion. All questions should be encouraged and answered in a courteous manner. Listen attentively to others without interrupting and be slow to judge. Be careful with sentences that start with "You should …" or "You ought …" and do not give unsolicited advice.

PRIORITY: Make the small group meeting a priority in your schedule. If you're unable to attend or are running late, call your group leader.

PREPAREDNESS: Prepare your lesson and come ready to share. What you put into the lesson is what you'll get out of it!

PARTICIPATION: Participate in the discussion, but keep your answers brief enough that others can share as well. The principle of participation says, "If there are ten people in the group, share slightly less than one-tenth of the time. If there are eight, share slightly less than one-eighth of the time," etc.

HONESTY: When appropriate, offer suggestions for improving the study to the leader in private.

CONNECT: Seek to know and care for other group members in addition to sharing transparently about your own emotional, spiritual, and physical needs.

CARE: If a member misses a session, be sure someone in the group calls to see how they're doing and catch them up on what was missed.

SUPPORT: Actively support the mission and values of the small group study and follow the directions given by your leader. Refrain from gossip and criticism; if you have concerns or questions about a member's views or statements, communicate directly and privately with that person.

ABOUT YOUR GUIDES

GODQUEST HOST AND CO-AUTHOR

Sean McDowell is a gifted communicator, author, and teacher. He serves as head of the Bible department at Christian Valley Christian Schools in San Juan Capistrano, California, and in 2008 he received the city's Educator of the Year award. Having graduated *summa cum laude* from Talbot Theological Seminary, Sean is now pursuing a PhD from Southern Baptist Theological Seminary. In addition to traveling through the United States and abroad as a speaker, he is the co-author of a number of books, including *Is God Just a Human Invention?*, *Understanding Intelligent Design*, and *More Than a Carpenter*. Sean lives with his wife and two children in San Juan Capistrano. You can visit Sean online at **SeanMcDowell.org**

GODQUEST VIDEO GUIDES

In order of appearance

Barbara Wise is HIV positive and the co-founder, along with her husband, Rick, of WiseChoices, a nonprofit organization that presents their gripping story in order to educate audiences regarding HIV and AIDS, forming healthy relationships, and hope in marriage. WiseChoices' goal is to empower young people to make healthy choices about the high-risk behavior of teen sex. Barb and Rick speak throughout the world and have been featured on TV or radio in every state as well as in Europe, Africa, and South America. Barb graduated *cum laude* from the University of Denver with a bachelor's desgree in speech communications and served on the Presidential Advisory Council on HIV/ AIDS. Barb and Rick live in Colorado, and you can learn more about them and WiseChoices at **Wise-Choices.org**.

Dr. Craig J. Hazen is the founder and director of the master's program in Christian apologetics at Biola University. He is the editor of the journal *Philosophia Christi* and author of several books, including the acclaimed novel *Five Sacred Crossings*. Hazen holds a PhD from the University of California and has won a range of awards for his teaching, research, and writing.

He is a much-sought-after speaker and has even lectured in the White House and on Capitol Hill. To see a full list of his writings and lectures, visit **CraigHazen.com** or **Biola.edu/academics/sas/apologetics/faculty**.

Lee Strobel is the former award-winning legal editor of the *Chicago Tribune* and a *New York Times* best-selling author of more than twenty books, including his atheist-turned-Christian personal story in *The Case for Christ*. He has been interviewed on numerous national television networks, including ABC, Fox, PBS, and CNN. Described in *The Washington Post* as "one of the evangelical community's most popular apologists," Lee has written such bestselling books as *The Case for Faith*, *The Case for a Creator*, *The Case for the Real Jesus*, and his highly anticipated novel, *The Ambition*. Lee earned his bachelor's degree in journalism at the University of Missouri and a master's degree in law from Yale. He and his wife have two grown children and live in Colorado. Learn more at **LeeStrobel.com**.

Josh McDowell has given more than twenty-four thousand talks to over 10 million young people in 118 countries since beginning ministry in 1961. He is the author or co-author of 112 books, selling over 51 million copies worldwide, including *More Than a Carpenter* (15 million copies worldwide), which has been translated into over eighty-five languages, and *The New Evidence That Demands a Verdict*, recognized by *World* magazine as one of the century's top forty books. Josh is currently traveling the United States with the message of TRUTH in the context of RELATIONSHIPS. This message is designed to help adults and young people take their faith and scriptural beliefs to form solid convictions that will stand firm in the face of constant worldly attacks. Josh will tell you that his family does not come before his ministry—his family *is* his ministry. He and his wife, Dottie, have been married for forty years and have four children and five very precious grandchildren. Learn more about Josh and his ministry at **Josh.org**

Miles McPherson played four years in the NFL with the San Diego Chargers, from 1982 through 1985. After committing his life to Christ and overcoming an addiction to cocaine in one day, Miles went to work as a youth pastor and later received his master's of divinity degree from Azusa Pacific University. In 1992, McPherson founded Miles Ahead, a non-profit organization that reaches out to youth around the globe and has helped more than forty-five thousand young people give their lives to the Lord. In 2000, he founded The Rock Church, which has consistently been one of the nation's fastest-growing and largest churches. Miles' newest book, *DO Something!*, is designed to equip people to take Christ's love to the streets and make a difference in their communities. Miles and his wife, Debbie, have three children and reside in San Diego. Learn more at **MilesMcPherson.com**.

Dave Dravecky pitched seven years in Major League Baseball, playing as an All-Star and in two pennant races. In 1988, doctors diagnosed him with cancer, leading to the removal of half of the deltoid muscle in his pitching arm. Defying all odds, Dave came back to pitch a winning game for the San Francisco Giants, but the return of the cancer in 1989 resulted in the amputation of his pitching arm and shoulder. Dave is in great demand as a motivational speaker, and has written several books, including *Comeback*, *Called Up: Stories of Life and Faith from the Great Game of Baseball*, and *The Worth of a Man*. He and his wife, Jan, founded the nonprofit organization Endurance to help others endure the journey through cancer. Dave resides in Colorado with his wife, and he especially loves being a grandpa. Learn more about Dave and his ministry at **DaveDravecky.com** and **Endurance.org**.

Mark L. Strauss earned his PhD at Aberdeen and is professor of New Testament at Bethel Seminary in San Diego. He is the author and co-author of a number of books, including *Four Portraits, One Jesus: An Introduction to Jesus and the Gospels*, "Mark," in the revised *Expositor's Bible Commentary*, *The Essential Bible Companion*, and "Luke" in the *Zondervan Illustrated Bible Backgrounds Commentary*. He serves on the Committee for Bible Translation for the New International Version and is an associate editor of the *NIV Study Bible*. Mark preaches and teaches regularly at churches, conferences, and colleges and has served in three interim pastorates. He lives in San Diego with his wife, Roxanne, and three children. Read more online at **Bethel.edu/seminary/faculty/bssd/strauss**.

ABOUT YOUR GUIDES

GODQUEST

Greg Koukl is the founder and president of Stand to Reason ministry and the award-winning author of *Tactics: A Game Plan for Discussing Your Christian Convictions, Relativism: Feet Firmly Planted in Mid-Air* with Francis J. Beckwith, and *Precious Unborn Human Persons*. Greg received his master's in philosophy of religion and ethics at Talbot School of Theology, and his master's in christian apologetics from Simon Greenleaf University. He is an adjunct professor at Biola University and has hosted his own radio talk show for over twenty years. Greg has published more than 180 articles and has spoken on nearly sixty university and college campuses both in the U.S. and abroad. Visit Greg online and learn more about Stand to Reason at **STR.org**.

GODQUEST CO-AUTHOR

Jennifer Dion is the director of product development at Outreach Publishing and the bestselling author of the *Fireproof Your Marriage* curriculum materials. She does a lot of editing and writing for new books, church-wide campaigns, and small group curriculum, including *To Save A Family, The Grace Card Study Guide*, and more. Jennifer has a background in marketing, holding a bachelor's degree from The Ohio State University and an MBA from San Diego State University. She loves Bible history and archaeology and is pursuing a master's degree in apologetics from Biola University. Jennifer has twin daughters and a son and lives in beautiful San Diego County.

Then you will know
the truth,
and the truth
will set you free.

—John 8:32

SIGNPOST 1:

THE QUEST

WHAT YOU BELIEVE DETERMINES
WHERE YOU GO IN LIFE.

Quest: It means "to go on an adventurous journey in pursuit of something valuable." In this life, there's nothing more challenging, more enlightening, or more adventurous than pursuing truth. At some level, we're all on a quest for truth and understanding; we all have a set of beliefs about God, the meaning of life, and how the universe began. Unfortunately, we also live in a busy, fast-paced world, full of responsibilities and distractions. During His ministry, Jesus told a story to illustrate how the cares of the world can draw us away from God and His Word: *"The seed that fell among thorns stands for those who hear, but as they go on their way they are choked by life's worries, riches and pleasures, and they do not mature"* (Luke 8:14). As humans, we tend to focus on everyday concerns and reach out to God only when something goes wrong or something unexpected happens in our lives. If that's been true in your own life (even partially), then think about seeking God now—before things get off track.

For the next six weeks, you're invited to join us on a spiritual quest for a deeper understanding of something—or Someone—greater than ourselves. Together, we will explore some of the most pressing questions about God: Is there good reason to believe God exists? Can we trust the Bible? Why is there evil and suffering? Who was Jesus and is He really the only way to God?

We will encounter six Signposts on our spiritual journey. Signpost 1 reads, "What you believe determines where you go in life." That's an important concept because our beliefs affect our choices, the paths we take in life, and our ultimate destination. As you choose your path in life, you can decide either to seek God and follow after Him or set off on your own course.

Are you ready for a spiritual adventure? Are you ready for a *GodQuest*? Let's go!

Open your study with prayer.

Ask God to guide your thoughts and your words during your study. The Bible says God is a God of truth, so pray for Him to reveal truth as you watch the *GodQuest* video teaching, study the Bible, and answer this week's questions.

Starting Location

Before you begin any journey, you need to know your starting location. Use these first questions to find out where you are in your views on God.

If you're doing the *GodQuest* study with a group, you'll start each weekly meeting with an "icebreaker" question to jumpstart your discussion and help you get to know one another.

Icebreaker Question

Pretty much all of us have been lost at some point in our lives. Did you ever "lose" a parent in the grocery store? Wander off the marked trail during a hike? Try to drive through Boston during construction? Think of the worst, funniest, or most ridiculous experience you've had while lost and share it with your group.

_____

_____

_____

_____

TRAVEL TIP: Offer a prize for the person who shares the funniest or most outrageous story. Take a vote after everyone is done sharing.

QUESTION 1

How did you arrive at your beliefs about God and religion? Below and on the next page is a list of methods for gathering information about God. Rank them from 1 to 9 in order of importance, with 1 being the most important method you've used to learn the truth about God and 9 being the least important.

__✓__ Going to church

__✓__ Reading the Bible

GODQUEST

✓ Talking with friends

✳ Reading books or watching TV programs on religion

___ Using the Internet (reading websites, downloading podcasts, etc.)

___ Prayer

___ Listening to my parents and other members of my family

✗ Having a spiritual experience *?*

✗ Other ___MUSIC_____

When you're done, share your answers with your group.

QUESTION 2

Indicate your level of agreement with the following statements:

I've investigated more than one religion (for example, both Christianity and Islam).

✓ Strongly Agree ___ Agree ___ Uncertain ___ Disagree ___ Strongly Disagree

I've changed my religious beliefs at some point in my life.

✓ Strongly Agree ___ Agree ___ Uncertain ___ Disagree ___ Strongly Disagree

Religious views are subjective (personal opinion); one view is not more correct than another.

___ Strongly Agree ___ Agree ___ Uncertain ___ Disagree ___ Strongly Disagree

There is more than one way (and more than one religion) that leads to heaven.

___ Strongly Agree ✗ Agree ___ Uncertain ___ Disagree ___ Strongly Disagree

In order to go to heaven, people need to do good works in this life.

___ Strongly Agree ___ Agree ___ Uncertain ✗ Disagree ___ Strongly Disagree

When you're done, share your answers with your group.

TRAVEL TIP: As you listen to other people share their answers, remember that gentleness and respect are important characteristics for a good group discussion. Allow other group members to share without judging their answers or attempting to correct them.

Directions from Your Guides

Play the Signpost 1 video on the *GodQuest* Reources DVD.

After you watch the video lesson, answer the following questions. If you're doing *GodQuest* with a group, share your answers with the other group members.

QUESTION 3

What stood out to you in this week's video lesson? Why?

_____

_____

_____

_____

QUESTION 4

Dr. Hazen gave four reasons for starting a *GodQuest* by considering Christianity. Which of those reasons do you think is the most compelling? Why?

_____

_____

_____

_____

QUESTION 5

Sean listed some of the typical barriers to a *GodQuest*. Have you run into any of these barriers? If so, which ones?

_____

_____

_____

GODQUEST

TRAVEL TIP: You can watch Sean give an entire talk on the topic of beginning a religious quest in a video called "Why Any Serious Religious Quest Should Begin with Christianity" at his website, SeanMcDowell.org. You'll find the video on the "Curriculum" page.

Trip Planner

READ: Luke 15:3–7, 19:10, Romans 10:16–21

"For the Son of Man came to seek and to save what was lost." —Luke 19:10

MAP LEGEND:

In Luke 19:10, Jesus called Himself the "Son of Man." Jesus' use of that phrase didn't mean that He was merely human. Instead, it was a reference to Daniel 7:13–14, which reads, "In my vision at night I looked, and there before me was one like a *son of man*, coming with the clouds of heaven. He approached the Ancient of Days and was led into his presence. He was given authority, glory and sovereign power; all peoples, nations and men of every language worshiped him. His dominion is an everlasting dominion that will not pass away, and his kingdom is one that will never be destroyed." By referring to Himself as the "Son of Man," Jesus revealed that He was the one described in Daniel's prophecy—the Son of God whose kingdom is everlasting.

"I was found by those who did not seek me; I revealed myself to those who did not ask for me." —Romans 10:20

"Suppose one of you has a hundred sheep and loses one of them. Does he not leave the ninety-nine in the open country and go after the lost sheep until he finds it? And when he finds it, he joyfully puts it on his shoulders and goes home." —Luke 15:4–6

QUESTION 6

So far in this study, we've been talking about seeking God, but after reading these passages, who do you think is seeking whom? Does God make the first move to create a relationship with us, or are we reaching out to Him?

_____

_____

_____

_____

QUESTION 7

How do you feel about the statement that God wants to have a relationship with you? Exodus 34:14 even says God is jealous about His relationship with you. See the verse below.

_____

_____

_____

_____

"You must worship no other gods, for the LORD, whose very name is Jealous, is a God who is jealous about his relationship with you." —Exodus 34:14 (NLT)

READ: Luke 11:9–13, Hebrews 11:6, James 4:7–8

"So I say to you: Ask and it will be given to you; seek and you will find; knock and the door will be opened to you. For everyone who asks receives; he who seeks finds; and to him who knocks, the door will be opened." —Luke 11:9–10

And without faith it is impossible to please God, because anyone who comes to him must believe that he exists and that he rewards those who earnestly seek him. —Hebrews 11:6

Submit yourselves, then, to God. Resist the devil, and he will flee from you. Come near to God and he will come near to you. —James 4:7–8

QUESTION 8

According to these verses, how does God respond to those who desire a relationship with Him?

_____

_____

_____

_____

GODQUEST

QUESTION 9

The James 4 passage says we are to *"come near to God."* How would you describe your current relationship with God—how "near" are you to Him? What steps could you take to draw closer, and what has kept you from taking those steps?

_____

_____

_____

_____

Close your weekly study with prayer. If you're doing the *GodQuest* study in a group, ask group members to share prayer requests; then close your group meeting in prayer.

BEFORE NEXT WEEK'S STUDY, BE SURE TO COMPLETE *THE WEEKLY QUEST* AND THE DAILY *TRAVEL LOGS*.

If you would like to dig deeper into the topics from this week, read Signpost 1 in the *GodQuest* nonfiction book by Sean McDowell and Stan Jantz.

The Weekly Quest

The objective of the *GodQuest* study is not to tell you what to think, but rather to challenge and encourage you to go on a real spiritual quest of your own. To help you with your quest, this section of your Guidebook will have suggestions about websites you can visit, topics you can research, and books, videos, or movies that will challenge your thinking and help you build a strong foundation for your faith.

TRAVEL TIP: If you would like to learn more about Barbara and Rick Wise and their ministry, you can find them at Wise-Choices.org. Your other guide for this week, Dr. Craig Hazen, is the director of apologetics at Biola University. You can read more about the study of apologetics at Biola.edu/academics/sas/apologetics, or simply do a search on "Biola apologetics."

This week, we've given you some information about two of your video guides, but rather than suggest a lot of places for you to visit, we first want to help you determine where you *are*. When you plan a trip (or get directions from a map site), you need to know two things: your destination and your starting location. In the case of a spiritual journey, your starting location is your current understanding of God and your relationship with Him. In Matthew 13, Jesus told a story that will help you get a feel for your spiritual *location*.

READ: Matthew 13:1–9, 18–23

Jesus described four places on which seed fell. Think about these Bible passages and then read the four descriptions below. Which one best describes where you are with God?

THE PATH: Have you heard God's Word but have either not understood it or rejected it? *"When anyone hears the message about the kingdom and does not understand it, the evil one comes and snatches away what was sown in his heart"* (Matthew 13:19).

THE ROCKY PLACES: Have you accepted God's Word but not developed a deep, long-term faith? Did your relationship with Jesus only last a short time before you drifted away? *"The one who received the seed that fell on rocky places is the man who hears the word and at once receives it with joy. But since he has no root, he lasts only a short time. When trouble or persecution comes because of the word, he quickly falls away"* (Matthew 13:20–21).

THE THORNS: Have you accepted God's Word but then allowed the worries and busyness of life to distract you and keep you from building a strong, productive faith? Would you say your life is producing "fruit" in God's kingdom, or would you instead admit that you feel busy and immersed in the daily challenges of the world? *"The one who received the seed that fell among the thorns is the man who hears the word, but the worries of this life and the deceitfulness of wealth choke it, making it unfruitful"* (Matthew 13:22).

THE GOOD SOIL: Have you accepted God's Word and then steadily grown in your faith and brought other people to Christ? Does your faith encourage others to seek God and to have the kind of peace and purpose they see in your life? *"But the one who received the seed that fell on good soil is the man who hears the word and understands it. He produces a crop, yielding a hundred, sixty or thirty times what was sown"* (Matthew 13:23).

If you're on the good soil, pray for God to use this study to help you add to your knowledge and grow your ability to reach others for His kingdom. If you're on the *path*, the *rocky places*, or among the *thorns*, this is your opportunity to seek a closer, more fruitful relationship with God. Do you remember the Bible passages we studied about how God responds to those who seek Him? Take this time to pray and ask God to reveal Himself to you through this study. If you have doubts or questions, share those with God. If you've succumbed to the pressures of life and allowed those to pull you away from God, confess this to Him and commit to drawing near to Him during this study.

Use the space below to write out your prayer.

_____

_____

_____

_____

_____

_____

_____

TRAVEL LOGS

DAY 1

Listen, my son, and be wise, and keep your heart on the right path.
—Proverbs 23:19

Draw a spiritual "map" of your life in the space below. Draw a starting point to indicate your birth; then draw a line to show the course of your life. Change the direction of the line to indicate when your life went in a different direction (for example, you started or ended an important relationship, something big happened to you, you moved or took a new job, etc.). Add a few notes beside the line sections to indicate what was happening in your life.

When you're done, spend some time thinking about the course of your life. In particular, think about the times when you made an important choice or when something big happened. At each of those critical times, what did you believe about right and wrong? What did you feel was the purpose of your life? How did your view of God affect your choices or your response to the events in your life?

You were running a good race. Who cut in on you and kept you from obeying the truth? That kind of persuasion does not come from the one who calls you. "A little yeast works through the whole batch of dough." I am confident in the Lord that you will take no other view. The one who is throwing you into confusion will pay the penalty, whoever he may be. —Galatians 5:7–10

Did You Know?

The Barna Group, an organization that researches religious beliefs in America, recently released a study on the diversity of faith among cities across the nation. The study clearly showed that religious beliefs greatly vary from city to city. For example, when survey respondents were asked to agree or disagree with the statement, "The Bible is accurate in all of the principles it teaches," 73 percent of the residents of Charlotte, North Carolina, agreed, in comparison to only 27 percent of the residents of San Francisco. In Birmingham, Alabama, 67 percent of the residents attend church on a weekly basis, but in Portland, Maine, 43 percent of the residents had not been to a religious worship service in the last six months.[1]

Why do you think religious beliefs vary so greatly from city to city?

_____

_____

_____

_____

Reread Galatians 5:7–10 at the top of the previous page. In what ways do people influence each other? How is that influence like yeast in a batch of dough?

_____

_____

_____

_____

When it comes to spiritual beliefs, would you say you are *influenced* or you are an *influencer*? What would help you stand firm in your beliefs?

_____

_____

_____

_____

WANT MORE? Go to Barna.org to read more studies and learn about trends relating to religious beliefs.

[1] "New Barna Report Examines Diversity of Faith in Various U.S. Cities," available from Barna.org, October 11, 2010.

GodQuest Profile: C. S. Lewis

C. S. Lewis, who lived from 1898–1963, was a brilliant teacher, author, and apologist (someone who defends the Christian faith). You might know him as the author of *The Lion, the Witch and the Wardrobe*; *Prince Caspian*; and the rest of *The Chronicles of Narnia*. In addition to the stories of Narnia, Lewis also wrote *Mere Christianity*, *The Screwtape Letters*, and other influential books about the truth of Christianity. But if you read about the first part of his life, you might be surprised that he became such a staunch defender of the Christian faith. Although he grew up in a family with Christian beliefs, at fifteen Lewis turned away from his childhood faith and became an atheist. He was very intelligent, and when he became an adult, he pursued academic interests, attending prestigious Oxford University and then later teaching at both Oxford and Cambridge.

Even as a professed atheist, Lewis' curiosity and intellect caused him to seek the truth about God. He was drawn to God yet resistant to surrendering control of his life to an all-powerful Lord. In *Surprised by Joy*, Lewis' story of his own life, he wrote, "A young man who wishes to remain a sound atheist cannot be too careful of his reading. There are traps everywhere … God is, if I may say it, very unscrupulous."[2] He continued to be drawn toward God, and in his book, Lewis described how he finally succumbed to God's pursuit: "Night after night, [I felt], whenever my mind lifted even for a second from my work, the steady, unrelenting approach of Him whom I so earnestly desired not to meet. That which I greatly feared had at last come upon me. In the Trinity Term of 1929 I gave in, and admitted that God was God, and knelt and prayed: perhaps, that night, the most dejected and reluctant convert in all England."[3]

[2] C. S. Lewis, *Surprised by Joy* (London: Fount, 1977), 153-4.
[3] Ibid., 95.

Lewis described himself as a "reluctant convert." What are some of the reasons people have for resisting God and avoiding a relationship with Him?

_____

_____

_____

_____

_____

_____

_____

_____

Have you ever been reluctant to search for God or to give Him control of your life? What were your reasons, and how did that reluctance impact your life?

_____

_____

_____

_____

_____

_____

WANT MORE? Go to CSLewis.com to read more about Lewis' life and writings. You can find his books online or at most bookstores.

DAY 4

Read the first six lines of "The Road Not Taken," a poem by Robert Frost:

> *Two roads diverged in a yellow wood,*
>
> *And sorry I could not travel both*
>
> *And be one traveler, long I stood*
>
> *And looked down one as far as I could*
>
> *To where it bent in the undergrowth;*
>
> *Then took the other, as just as fair.*

Have you ever faced this type of dilemma in your personal decisions and been confronted with two or more competing choices? In this kind of situation, how do any of us choose the right path? The Bible offers an answer: *Trust in the* LORD *with all your heart and lean not on your own understanding; in all your ways acknowledge him, and he will make your paths straight (Proverbs 3:5–6).*

When you're faced with a difficult choice in life, what are some of the things that influence your decision making?

Does it fit with my belief system?
Does it feel compelling?
What do trusted confidants think?
Is it "reversible"? - ie. if it does not
  work out, can the decision be changed?
Ben Franklin list.

Read the end of "The Road Not Taken":

> Oh, I marked the first for another day!
> Yet knowing how way leads on to way
> I doubted if I should ever come back.
>
> I shall be telling this with a sigh
> Somewhere ages and ages hence:
> Two roads diverged in a wood, and I,
> I took the one less traveled by,
> And that has made all the difference.[4]

Is there a choice you've made in your life that you wish you could take back? How would you choose differently?

_____

_____

_____

_____

_____

[4] Robert Frost, *Selected Poems of Robert Frost* (New York: Holt, Rinehart and Winston, Inc., 1963), 71.

Reflections from Your Journey

Each week, when you reach this section of your Guidebook, spend some time thinking about what you've learned; then reflect on your own spiritual journey.

As you think back over the video teaching, discussion questions, and *Travel Logs* from this week, what made the biggest impression on you? Why?

_____

_____

_____

_____

_____

_____

Was there anything that surprised you? What was it and why?

_____

_____

_____

_____

_____

_____

_____

Now, list some adjectives that best describe your current relationship with God (for example, *comforting, inconsistent, powerful, nonexistent, loving,* etc.).

_____

_____

_____

_____

_____

What would you most like to take away from this study? Below, list a few of those goals.

_____

_____

_____

_____

Finish this week's study by spending some time in prayer. Lay before God any pain or guilt you have over bad decisions from your past. Ask Him to reveal Himself to you as you go through *GodQuest*. Share with Him your goals for this study and pray that He would help you achieve those goals.

If you don't have a relationship with Jesus Christ, you can start one today. If you're doing *GodQuest* in a group, talk with your group leader about accepting Christ into your life. If you're doing *GodQuest* on your own, talk with a pastor or Christian friend.

Next Week: "The Beginning"

What you believe about creation determines how you view yourself and life.

In the beginning
God created the heavens
and the earth.

—Genesis 1:1

SIGNPOST 2:
THE BEGINNING
WHAT YOU BELIEVE ABOUT CREATION DETERMINES HOW YOU VIEW YOURSELF AND LIFE.

On a clear night this week, go outside, tip your head back, and look up into the sky. As you look at the beautiful array of stars, many of them trillions of miles away from your home on earth, how do you feel? Do you suddenly feel tiny, or maybe awestruck by the immeasurable universe? Three thousand years ago, Israel's King David looked up at the stars and said this: *"When I consider your heavens, the work of your fingers, the moon and the stars, which you have set in place, what is man that you are mindful of him, the son of man that you care for him?" (Psalm 8:3–4).* The prophet Isaiah said something very similar: "Lift your eyes and look to the heavens: Who created all these? *He who brings out the starry host one by one, and calls them each by name" (Isaiah 40:26).* David and Isaiah both believed the star-filled night sky indicated the presence of a powerful Creator. Since then, each successive generation has gazed at the skies, pondered the origin of the universe, and considered the existence of God.

This week, our topic is the origin of the universe and all living things. During our study, we will encounter Signpost 2, which says that what you believe about creation determines how you view yourself and life. Have you been taught that your life is the chance product of a vast and purposeless universe? Or have you gazed at the beauty of the star-filled sky and believed that an intelligent Creator designed the universe and then gave you life? Depending on what you believe, you will either seek to know your Creator or decide there is no Creator and go your own way.

Let's step backward in time and take look at "The Beginning." Are you ready to be amazed?

Open your study with prayer.

Starting Location

Before you begin any journey, you need to know your starting location. Use these first questions to find where you are in your views on God. If you're doing *GodQuest* with a group, share your answers with the other group members.

Icebreaker Question

Take a minute and think about the world you live in—its geographical characteristics and the plants, animals, and people around you. What is one thing about the world that amazes you? For example, is there a place you've visited (such as the Grand Canyon), a human capability, a characteristic of a favorite animal, or a scientific truth that just takes your breath away?

_____

_____

_____

_____

QUESTION 1

When you were in school, what did you learn about the origin of the universe and how life began? Were you taught anything different by your parents or at church? If so, how did you reconcile the different views?

_____

_____

_____

_____

QUESTION 2

Indicate your level of agreement with the following statements:

The universe is too organized and complex for it to have originated on its own. It must have had a Creator.

___ Strongly Agree ___ Agree ___ Uncertain ___ Disagree ___ Strongly Disagree

The universe has always existed.

___ Strongly Agree ___ Agree ___ Uncertain ___ Disagree ___ Strongly Disagree

Life began with very simple life forms (such as single-cell organisms) and then evolved by purely natural means to the complex species that exist today.

___ Strongly Agree ___ Agree ___ Uncertain ___ Disagree ___ Strongly Disagree

When you're done, share your answers with your group. If you're doing *GodQuest* on your own, find a friend and ask them to answer questions 1 and 2. How do your answers compare?

_____

_____

_____

_____

TRAVEL TIP: Remember, this section of the study is intended to help you determine your current beliefs and to initiate discussion with your group. Let the other group members share their answers without arguing or attempting to correct them.

Directions from Your Guides

Play the Signpost 2 video on your *GodQuest* Resource DVD.

After you watch the video lesson, answer the following questions. If you're doing *GodQuest* with a group, share your answers with the other group members.

QUESTION 3

What stood out to you in this week's video lesson? Why?

_____

_____

_____

QUESTION 4

How did Lee Strobel's beliefs regarding God and creation impact his decisions and the course of his life? Now, think about your own life. Have you ever been at a specific point in life when your views about creation directly affected your life journey?

_____

_____

QUESTION 5

In his teaching, Sean raised the question, What *best* explains the source for the information in DNA? How would you answer Sean? Explain the reason(s) behind your answer.

_____

_____

_____

GODQUEST

Trip Planner

READ: Isaiah 40:25–26, Job 38:31–32

"To whom will you compare me? Or who is my equal?" says the Holy One. Lift your eyes and look to the heavens: Who created all these? He who brings out the starry host one by one and calls them each by name. —Isaiah 40:25–26

"Can you bind the beautiful Pleiades? Can you loose the cords of Orion? Can you bring forth the constellations in their seasons or lead out the Bear with its cubs?" —Job 38:31–32

MAP LEGEND:

Pleiades is a cluster of stars also referred to as the Seven Sisters. Orion is a constellation known as the Hunter because of the visual picture its stars create. "The Bear with its cubs" are Ursa Major and Ursa Minor—constellations that form the shape of a large and small bear. You might also know some of the stars in these two constellations as the Big Dipper and the Little Dipper. All three of these constellations are visible from the earth, so if you look at the sky tonight, you might see the beautiful Pleiades, Orion, or the Bear with its cubs!

QUESTION 6

Carl Sagan, an atheist and the producer of the TV show *Cosmos*, once viewed a picture of the earth taken from space and said, "Our posturings, our imagined self-importance, the delusion that we have some privileged position in the universe, are challenged by this point of pale light. Our planet is a lonely speck in the great enveloping cosmic dark. In our obscurity, in all this vastness, there is no hint that help will come from elsewhere to save us from ourselves." Compare Sagan's viewpoint with Isaiah's (in the passage you just read). Which of the two quotes most closely matches your own views? Why?

_____

_____

_____

_____

_____

READ: Romans 1:18–20, Psalm 19:1–2

The wrath of God is being revealed from heaven against all the godlessness and wickedness of men who suppress the truth by their wickedness, since what may be known about God is plain to them, because God has made it plain to them. For since the creation of the world God's invisible qualities—his eternal power and divine nature—have been clearly seen, being understood from what has been made, so that men are without excuse. —Romans 1:18–20

The heavens declare the glory of God; the skies proclaim the work of his hands. Day after day they pour forth speech; night after night they display knowledge. —Psalm 19:1–2

QUESTION 7

In what ways does the universe, including its physical characteristics and living creatures, indicate the presence or absence of a Creator?

_____

_____

_____

_____

QUESTION 8

According to these verses, are you responsible for your belief (or lack of belief) in God, even if no one ever taught you about God or invited you to church? What's your reaction to the statements in Romans 1:18–20?

_____

_____

_____

_____

GODQUEST

READ: Genesis 1:27, Psalm 139:13–14

So God created man in his own image, in the image of God he created him; male and female he created them. —Genesis 1:27

For you created my inmost being; you knit me together in my mother's womb. I praise you because I am fearfully and wonderfully made; your works are wonderful, I know that full well. —Psalm 139:13–14

Question 9

Psalm 139 was written by Israel's King David, who praised God for His incredible power and knowledge—but also for His abilities as Creator. Consider the complexity and resilience of the human body. What about your body (and the human body in general) is indeed "fearfully and wonderfully made"?

_____

_____

_____

_____

Close your weekly study with prayer. If you're doing the *GodQuest* study in a group, ask group members to share prayer requests; then close your group meeting in prayer.

BEFORE NEXT WEEK'S STUDY, BE SURE TO COMPLETE *THE WEEKLY QUEST* AND THE DAILY *TRAVEL LOGS.*

If you would like to dig deeper into the topics from this week, read Signpost 2 in the *GodQuest* nonfiction book by Sean McDowell and Stan Jantz.

The Weekly Quest

Many of the resources for this week cover a number of topics related to intelligent design and creation. Rather than being organized by topics below, they are arranged by type: websites, books, and videos. Read through the descriptions and then pick at least one or two websites to visit. You could also stop by a local bookstore and pick up a new book, order one of the resources online, or read a sample chapter or review.

Challenge yourself to spend some time this week reviewing what experts say about intelligent design, the age of the earth, Darwin's theories, and the characteristics of life and the universe.

INTELLIGENT DESIGN

Websites:

- **LeeStrobel.com.** Lee's website includes videos and interviews with leading experts on intelligent design, along with other topics relating to the truth of Christianity. At the top of the website, look for "Video Channels" and then select "Investigating God." You can also purchase a copy of Lee's book *The Case for a Creator* through the site's store.

- **SeanMcDowell.org.** Sean's website features videos, articles, and a blog. Watch Sean's recent speaking engagements and debates or post a blog on an argument for the existence of God. Sean's articles and stories are current, feature teaching and comments from topical experts, and include replies from both sides of the debate. In addition, you can watch Sean expand on the evidence for a Creator in his talk "Understanding Intelligent Design", available for free on his website. Sean's site also includes links to books and resources.

- **Probe.org.** Probe Ministries' website contains a long list of articles relating to Christianity. To read the articles on the origin of the universe, select "Faith and Science" and then "Origins." You'll find articles on Darwin's theories, fossils, the fine-tuning of the universe, DNA, and more.

- **Reasons.org.** Reasons To Believe bridges the gap between science and faith by exploring questions about God and the Bible and providing resources on topics like creationism, intelligent design, prophecy and the end times, the age of the earth,* the Garden of Eden, heaven and hell, and Christian apologetics. You'll find podcasts, videos, a blog, printed publications, and a store with a number of resources.

- **ICR.org.** For four decades, the Institute for Creation Research has equipped believers with evidence of the Bible's accuracy and authority through scientific research, educational programs, and media presentations, all conducted within a thoroughly biblical framework. ICR's website includes articles, videos, and a store with books and audio CDs.

   Note: Christians have differing opinions on the age of the earth. We've included websites that cover the different views, so take some time to read the evidence and decide for yourself.

Books:

- *The Case for a Creator* by Lee Strobel. Join Lee Strobel as he reexamines the theories that once led him away from God. Through his compelling account, you'll encounter mind-stretching discoveries in cosmology, cellular biology, DNA, and human consciousness that present astonishing evidence for a Creator.

- *Understanding Intelligent Design* by William A. Dembski and Sean McDowell. This compact guide breaks down the core beliefs of intelligent design, explaining the central theories of intelligent design and showing why scientific evidence increasingly conflicts with evolutionary theories. It also points out how both evolution and intelligent design have radical implications for our culture and what readers can do about it.

- *Creation and Evolution 101* by Bruce Bickel and Stan Jantz. Simple yet comprehensive, this witty guide offers insights on the theory of evolution, including modern scientific evidence indicating intelligent design, the Christian approach to science, and Genesis and the latest findings. Learn to think clearly about the facts and opinions of science and how they can influence our understanding of the Bible.

- *Signature in the Cell: DNA and the Evidence for Intelligent Design* by Stephen C. Meyer (PhD in the philosophy of science, Cambridge).This book presents the first attempt to argue for intelligent design based upon what can be observed and documented in DNA.

  Note: This is an intermediate-level book, while some of the other books listed here are more introductory in nature.

- *The Genesis Debate* by J. Ligon Duncan III, David W. Hall, Hugh Ross, Gleason L. Archer, Lee Irons, Meredith G. Kline, and editor David G. Hagopian. Are the Genesis creation days twenty-fours hours long? Ages of time? Or a literary framework? In *The Genesis Debate*, three teams of evangelicals committed to the infallibility and inerrancy of Scripture tackle this question head-on by presenting and defending their respective views in a lively yet friendly forum.

GODQUEST

Videos:

- Illustra Media produces video documentaries that examine the scientific case for intelligent design. Working with Discovery Institute and an international team of scientists and scholars, Illustra has helped define both the scientific case for design and the limitations of materialistic processes like Darwinian evolution. These documentaries include *Unlocking the Mystery of Life*, *The Privileged Planet*, and *Darwin's Dilemma*. Illustra Media supplied some of the video you saw in this week's video. For more information, visit IllustraMedia.com.

- *Expelled: No Intelligence Allowed* Ben Stein may not look like a typical school rebel—but when he learned that educators and scientists were being ridiculed, denied tenure, and even fired for the "crime" of discussing evidence of design in nature, he'd had enough! Join him as he travels the world questioning academia's doctrine of random evolution and championing intellectual freedom! Also includes pocket-sized book of quotes.

- *Journey Inside the Cell.* Search YouTube.com.

Travel Logs

DAY 1

"Where were you when I laid the earth's foundation? Tell me, if you understand. Who marked off its dimensions? Surely you know! Who stretched a measuring line across it?" —Job 38:4–5

In their book *I Don't Have Enough Faith to Be an Atheist*, Frank Turek and Norman Geisler provide an explanation that might help you grasp the sheer size of the universe:

> There are 100 billion stars in our galaxy, and the average distance between those stars is 30 trillion miles. How far is 30 trillion miles? Let's put it this way: when the Space Shuttle is in orbit it travels at about 17,000 mph—*almost five miles per second*. If you could get in the Space Shuttle and speed through space at five miles per second, it would take you 201,450 years to travel 30 trillion miles! In other words, if you had gotten into the Space Shuttle at the time of Christ ... you would be only *one-hundredth* of the way there right now.[1]

Now, keep in mind that's just between two of the 100 billion stars in our galaxy. The distance across our galaxy is one hundred thousand light years. How many stars are there in the entire universe? *The number of stars in the universe is about equal to the number of sand grains on all the beaches on all the earth.* And at five miles per second it will take you over two hundred thousand years to go from one grain of sand to another. The heavens are awesome!

In Isaiah 40:12, the Bible says that God measures the heavens with the "breadth of his hand." What does it mean to you to have a Creator who is responsible for such a colossal, astonishing universe? Below, write a prayer to God praising Him for His creation.

_____

_____

_____

_____

_____

_____

_____

_____

_____

_____

_____

_____

_____

_____

[1] Norman L. Geisler and Frank Turek, *I Don't Have Enough Faith to Be an Atheist* (Wheaton, Illinois: Crossway Books, 2004), 153.

DAY 2

(Courtesy of Stan Jantz. Excerpted from *Creation and Evolution 101* by Bruce Bickel and Stan Jantz.)

Christians hold to different views regarding the age of the earth, but all three of the views listed here share the following essential beliefs:

- God created the universe.
- The Bible is the completely true Word of God.
- Our knowledge of God and His ways is incomplete.

Young-Earth Creationism

This is the view that God created the universe approximately six to ten thousand years ago in a period of six literal twenty-four-hour days. According to this view, the reason the earth "looks" much older than it is can be explained primarily by Noah's global flood (Genesis 6–8), which dramatically changed the geology of the earth. Young-earth creationists interpret the creation accounts in Genesis 1 and 2 literally.

Old-Earth Creationism

Also known as progressive creationism, this view is that God created the universe ten to fifteen billion years ago. While the Bible doesn't give us the age of the earth or the universe, it does tell us that time is different for God than for us (Psalm 90:4, 1 John 2:18). Those who hold this view interpret scientific evidence as pointing more and more to an old universe.

Theistic Evolution

In a nutshell, theistic evolutionists believe that God created human beings by means of evolution and natural selection. Although they believe the Bible is true, they interpret the creation accounts in the Bible in a figurative rather than literal way.

The Real Issue

As important as this issue is, it's not the real issue of creation. The much bigger and more important issue is whether God created the heavens and the earth. It's OK to be unsettled in your view of when creation happened, but don't let that distract you from the real issue.

Which of these views is closest to your own beliefs? Why do you think that view is the most reasonable, likely explanation for creation?

_____

_____

_____

_____

_____

_____

_____

_____

_____

_____

_____

_____

DAY 3

"Does the hawk take flight by your wisdom and spread his wings toward the south? Does the eagle soar at your command and build his nest on high?"
—Job 39:26–27

Did You Know?

Every autumn, beautiful monarch butterflies migrate from their northern homes to warmer areas in Southern California and Mexico. The butterflies travel approximately twenty-five hundred miles for up to two months, and they not only migrate to the same area each year—they actually migrate to the same trees! What's even more amazing is that the migrating butterflies have *never been* to the areas to which they're traveling! Each year, there are four generations of monarch butterflies. Three of the generations live for approximately two months. The other generation lives for six to eight months, and these are the butterflies that migrate to the warmer climate. They're "returning" to trees last visited by monarch butterflies three generations back!

The arctic tern migrates from the Arctic to the Antarctic and back again every year—a round-trip of forty-four thousand miles. This means that in its twenty-year lifespan, a single arctic tern will travel the equivalent of three round-trips to the moon!

Scientists have not been able to explain the amazing migration habits of these two species other than to say they migrate by *instinct*. This leaves one big, unanswered question: what—or Who—designed these migratory animals with such amazing *instincts*?

How do you think monarch butterflies and arctic terns know when to leave and where to go? How do the butterflies find the same trees every year?

_____

_____

_____

_____

_____

_____

_____

How does Job 39 explain migration?

_____

_____

_____

_____

_____

_____

_____

WANT MORE? Search for the DVD _Amazing Journeys—IMAX_ at IMAX.com

Amazing Journeys captures the life-and-death dramas of the incredible journeys of monarch butterflies, migratory birds, gray whales, red crabs, and zebras.

DAY 4

For since the creation of the world God's invisible qualities—his eternal power and divine nature—have been clearly seen, being understood from what has been made ... —Romans 1:20

"Do you give the horse his strength or clothe his neck with a flowing mane? ... He paws fiercely, rejoicing in his strength, and charges into the fray." —Job 39:19, 21

So far this week, you've watched a video about the unique properties of the universe and the incredible complexity of DNA. You've also read about the mind-boggling size of the universe and the inexplicable nature of animal instinct. If God created the universe and the unique, intricate life within it, then what does creation reveal about God? Who is He, and what is He like? Does He love beauty? Does He pay attention to detail? Does He have a sense of humor? What do you think?

Spend a little time looking at the photos on this page and considering what you know of the earth and the rest of the universe. Then, describe God. Below, list some adjectives or write a paragraph or even a short poem or psalm (song) to describe our Creator.

Reflections from Your Journey

As you think back over the video teaching, discussion questions, and *Travel Logs* from this week, what made the biggest impression on you? Why?

_____

_____

_____

_____

_____

_____

In what ways do your beliefs about creation affect how you view yourself and how you view life?

_____

_____

_____

_____

_____

In this week's study, what was the most compelling evidence for the existence of a loving Creator?

_____

_____

_____

_____

_____

_____

_____

If you were *very* confident that the universe—and you—were created by God,
how would that impact your life? Would you share that truth with other
people in your life? Would it change how you spend your time or even what
you do with your life? If you are *already sure*, how does that truth affect you?

_____

_____

_____

_____

_____

_____

Finish this week's study by spending some time in prayer. Praise God
for who He is and what He has created. Thank Him for creating you in a
fearful and wonderful way. Ask him to continue to reveal Himself to you as
you go through *GodQuest*. Commit to Him how you will share your faith
with others.

Next Week: "The Word"

What you believe about the Bible determines how you
live your life.

From infancy you have known the holy Scriptures, which are able to make you wise for salvation through faith in Christ Jesus. All Scripture is God-breathed and is useful for teaching, rebuking, correcting and training in righteousness, so that the man of God may be thoroughly equipped for every good work.

—2 Timothy 3:15–17

SIGNPOST 3:
THE WORD
WHAT YOU BELIEVE ABOUT THE BIBLE DETERMINES HOW YOU LIVE YOUR LIFE.

If you buy a new computer, smart phone, DVD player, or other electronic device, after sifting through the packaging you will find an owner's guide. Providing instructions for a sophisticated product is so typical, we know that when we open the box, the manual will be there. But life is far more complex than even the latest device from Apple, so where is the owner's manual?

The Apostle Paul gave his young protégé, Timothy, some life instructions in this week's key Bible passage, 2 Timothy 3:15–17. Paul pointed out several characteristics of the Bible: it will make us wise, it was inspired by God ("God-breathed"), and it will teach us, correct us, rebuke us, and train us. And the end result of studying the Bible is not only that we will be ready to handle life, but also that we will be thoroughly equipped for good works. In other words, by following the Bible, we can live lives of wisdom, purpose, and impact—lives that can change the world.

This week, we're going to explore the authenticity, accuracy, and purpose of the Bible. We're also going to encounter Signpost 3, which reads, "What you believe about the Bible determines how you live your life." If you believe the Bible is true, then you have an inspired, flawless, incredibly wise guidebook that will keep you on the right path in life. If you don't believe the Bible is true, then you'll need to decide on your own rules and your own map for life.

Let's take a look at "The Word."

Open your study with prayer.

Ask God to guide your thoughts and your words during your study. The Bible says God is a God of truth, so pray for Him to reveal truth as you watch the *GodQuest* video teaching, study the Bible, and answer this week's questions.

Starting Location

Use these first questions to find out *where you are* in your views on the Bible.

Icebreaker Question

Reflect on a book that had an effect on your thinking, your career, your finances, your relationships, or even a key decision in your life. What was that book, and why did it affect you? Share your answer if you are studying with a group.

_____

_____

_____

_____

TRAVEL TIP: Think about having a book exchange. If you still have a copy of the book you mentioned, offer to share it with someone in your group. Is there a book another group member described that interests you? Maybe they would let you borrow it.

QUESTION 1

Below and on the next page is a list of ways in which the Bible can affect you and the course of your life. Rank them from 1 to 7 in order of importance to you, with 1 being the most important and 7 the least important. Even if all of them seem important, try to rank them in the order in which they impact *you*.

The Bible:

___ Brings me comfort

___ Gives me wisdom for making decisions

GODQUEST

___ Lifts my spirit and brings me joy

___ Helps me understand God and His character

___ Instructs me on right and wrong

___ Draws me closer to God

___ Tells me how to relate to other people in my life

When you're done, share your answers if you are studying with a group.

QUESTION 2

Below, select the answers that most accurately describe your Bible-reading habits and knowledge.

I read the Bible:

___ Every day ___ Most day ___ A few times a month ___ Rarely ___ Never

I memorize Bible verses and can recall them when I need their teaching and assurance.

___ Strongly Agree ___ Agree ___ Uncertain ___ Disagree ___ Strongly Disagree

I'm familiar with Bible history, from Genesis through the ministry of Jesus and the apostles.

___ Strongly Agree ___ Agree ___ Uncertain ___ Disagree ___ Strongly Disagree

I understand the fundamental teachings of Jesus and His apostles.

___ Strongly Agree ___ Agree ___ Uncertain ___ Disagree ___ Strongly Disagree

My understanding of right and wrong is based on the teachings of the Bible.

___ Strongly Agree ___ Agree ___ Uncertain ___ Disagree ___ Strongly Disagree

When you're done, share your answers if you are studying with a group.

TRAVEL TIP: As you listen to other people share their answers, remember that gentleness and respect are important characteristics for a good group discussion. Allow other group members to share without judging their answers or attempting to correct them.

Directions from Your Guides

Play the Signpost 3 video on your *GodQuest* Resource DVD.

After you watch the video lesson, answer the following questions. If you're doing *GodQuest* with a group, share your answers with the other group members.

QUESTION 3

What was your reaction to Josh McDowell's story about forgiving someone who had greatly sinned against him simply because the Bible said he should? Have you ever done anything difficult because of a biblical teaching or principle?

_____

_____

_____

_____

QUESTION 4

Sean gave evidence for the authenticity of the Bible. What is the most important reason you believe the Bible? If you're not yet sure the Bible is true, what causes you the greatest doubt? What would help you overcome that doubt?

_____

_____

_____

_____

TRAVEL TIP: You can watch Sean give an entire talk on the reliability of the New Testament at his website, SeanMcDowell.org. You'll find the video on the "Curriculum" page.

Trip Planner

READ: 2 Timothy 3:15–17

From infancy you have known the holy Scriptures, which are able to make you wise for salvation through faith in Christ Jesus. All Scripture is God-breathed and is useful for teaching, rebuking, correcting and training in righteousness, so that the man of God may be thoroughly equipped for every good work. —2 Timothy 3:15–17

QUESTION 5

In your own words, summarize how the Bible can help you live your life. Then, give a specific example from your own life of a time when the Scriptures helped you. How did the Bible teach you, correct your actions, or equip you for good work?

_____

_____

_____

_____

If you are still evaluating Christianity and the Bible, write down one or two characteristics listed in 2 Timothy 3:15–17 that most appeal to you. How specifically could those characteristics of the Bible affect you and change your life?

_____

_____

_____

_____

READ: Psalms 12:6, 119:89

And the words of the LORD are flawless, like silver refined in a furnace of clay, purified seven times. —Psalm 12:6

Your word, O LORD, is eternal; it stands firm in the heavens. —Psalm 119:89

QUESTION 6

What does the Bible say of itself? In the previous two verses, underline the words you think are important. According to Psalm 12:6, could part of the Bible be true and part false (or inaccurate)? Why or why not?

_____

_____

_____

READ: Proverbs 22:5, 8, Psalm 119:1, 9–11

In the paths of the wicked lie thorns and snares, but he who guards his soul stays far from them. —Proverbs 22:5

He who sows wickedness reaps trouble. —Proverbs 22:8

Blessed are they whose ways are blameless, who walk according to the law of the LORD. —Psalm 119:1

How can a young man keep his way pure? By living according to your word. I seek you with all my heart; do not let me stray from your commands. I have hidden your word in my heart that I might not sin against you. —Psalm 119:9–11

QUESTION 7

King Solomon, who wrote the book of Proverbs, is often described as the wisest man who ever lived. What do you think of the wisdom in Proverbs 22:5, 8? From what you've seen and experienced in life, does sin cause us to run into "thorns and snares" and suffer the consequences of our choices? Give an example of a time when that happened in your life or in the life of someone you know.

_____

_____

_____

GODQUEST

QUESTION 8

How can the Bible help you stay away from sin and evil? What do you need to do to benefit from the Bible's teaching on right and wrong?

_____

_____

_____

READ: 2 Timothy 4:3–4, Titus 1:9

For the time will come when men will not put up with sound doctrine. Instead, to suit their own desires, they will gather around them a great number of teachers to say what their itching ears want to hear. They will turn their ears away from the truth and turn aside to myths. —2 Timothy 4:3–4

He must hold firmly to the trustworthy message as it has been taught, so that he can encourage others by sound doctrine and refute those who oppose it. —Titus 1:9

MAP LEGEND:

Doctrine means a specific set of teachings and beliefs. In this case, *doctrine* refers to what is taught in the Bible. In the New Testament, the Apostles Paul and Peter frequently warned Christians about false beliefs and cautioned them not to stray from what they had been taught by Jesus and the apostles. Unfortunately, it was all too common for false doctrine and distorted teaching to creep into the church and lead believers astray. See 1 Timothy 1, 4, Titus 1, and 2 Peter 2 for examples of these warnings from Peter and Paul.

QUESTION 9

Do you think 2 Timothy 4:3–4 describes our world today? Based on these two verses, what is one of the most important reasons for consistently reading the Bible and understanding what it says?

_____

_____

_____

READ: Psalms 17:5, 119:32, 105

My steps have held to your paths; my feet have not slipped. —Psalm 17:5

I run in the path of your commands, for you have set my heart free. —Psalm 119:32

Your word is a lamp to my feet and a light for my path. —Psalm 119:105

QUESTION 10

Would you say that you are on the right path in your life? Why or why not?

_____

_____

_____

_____

If not, what can you do to change direction and get there? How do you think it would feel to be walking a good path in life?

_____

_____

_____

READ: Proverbs 3:5–6

*Trust in the LORD with all your heart and lean not on your own understanding;
in all your ways acknowledge him, and he will make your paths straight.*
—Proverbs 3:5–6

GODQUEST

QUESTION 11

Proverbs 3:5–6 is many Christians' favorite Bible passage due to its clear truth and encouraging promise. Would you say you lean on God or on your own understanding for most of the decisions in your life? Is there a specific area in your life where you feel God is calling you to trust Him and make a change or a key decision? What is that area, and what can you do to more fully acknowledge and trust God?

_____

_____

_____

_____

Remember, God can take you on an amazing adventure when you trust Him!

Close your weekly study with prayer. If you're doing the *GodQuest* study in a group, ask group members to share prayer requests; then close your group meeting in prayer.

BEFORE NEXT WEEK'S STUDY, BE SURE TO COMPLETE *THE WEEKLY QUEST* AND THE DAILY *TRAVEL LOGS.*

If you would like to dig deeper into the topics from this week, read Signpost 3 in the *GodQuest* nonfiction book by Sean McDowell and Stan Jantz.

The Weekly Quest

There are many books, websites, and organizations that can help you learn more about the Bible. To choose the best place to start, consider these questions:

- What biblical topics or time frames interest you the most?
- Do you have unanswered questions about the Bible? What are they?
- What intrigued you the most in this week's lesson?
- What doubts do you have (or have you had in the past) regarding the Bible?
- Are there questions other people have asked regarding the Bible that you've struggled to answer?

Following are some of the topics covered this week, along with suggested books, websites, and additional resources. Pick one or more topics and do a little research of your own. After you complete this week's *Travel Logs*, you might want to circle back to this section. The *Travel Logs* might arouse your curiosity about a specific topic.

BIBLE FACTS: DATES, AUTHORS, LOCATIONS, AND LANGUAGES

Books:

- *Zondervan Illustrated Bible Backgrounds Commentary Set* (Old Testament and New Testament sets are available.)
- *Knowing the Bible 101* by Bruce Bickel and Stan Jantz
- In addition, there are many Bible dictionaries, encyclopedias, commentaries, and handbooks available. Study Bibles also have excellent information. See your local Christian bookstore or search online.

Websites:

- **BibleGateway.com** features quick and thorough Bible-search capability based on passage, keyword, or topic. The site also offers online Bible dictionaries, commentaries, daily reading plans, and more.
- **BiblePlaces.com** features photographs and descriptions of sites in Israel, Jordan, Egypt, Turkey, and Greece, with an emphasis on biblical archaeology, geography, and history.

- **Biblica.com/bibles/faq** offers answers to frequently asked questions about the Bible.

Other Resources:

- Logos Bible software is available for PCs, Macs, and iPhones. See **Logos.com.**

BIBLE VERSIONS AND MANUSCRIPTS

Books:

- *The New Evidence That Demands a Verdict* by Josh McDowell
- *More Than a Carpenter* by Josh and Sean McDowell

Websites:

- **Josh.org** features articles, free downloads, audio and video content, and a store with books and other resources.
- **LeeStrobel.com** Choose "Investigating the Bible" from the "Video Channels" menu.

THE BIBLE AND ARCHAEOLOGY

Books:

- *NIV Archaeological Study Bible*
- *Archaeology and the Old Testament* by Alfred J. Hoerth

Websites:

- BibleArchaeology.org
- Bib-Arch.org
- AllAboutArchaeology.org

Other Resources:

- *Biblical Archaeology Review* magazine
- *Bible and Spade* magazine

THE DEAD SEA SCROLLS

Books:

• *Holman QuickSource Quide to the Dead Sea Scrolls* by Craig A. Evans

Websites:

• BiblePlaces.com/Qumran.htm
• Loc.gov/exhibits/scrolls/

GO TO ISRAEL!

For an adventurous quest to learn more about the Bible, nothing can beat a trip to Israel or other Bible sites in the Middle East! While I (Jennifer) was taking a class on Bible archaeology, I enviously listened to the professor talk about his experiences on archaeological digs and wondered, *Do people actually get to go do that?* In the summer of 2008, I found out when I spent two weeks on a combination tour and archaeological project centered in Jerusalem. I'll never forget literally sifting through some of the remains from the Temple Mount.

I (Sean) took a group of my students on an apologetics study tour to Israel in April 2011. You saw a little part of our trip in this week's video lesson. My highlight was our visit to Cave Four at Qumran, near the Dead Sea, where they found the Great Isaiah Scroll. It was also amazing to see the remains of Jericho, which testify to the biblical story of Joshua leading the Israelites into the Promised Land roughly 3,400 years ago. There is truly nothing like seeing firsthand the very places where Jesus walked and healed people. If you want the Bible to come alive, think about visiting the Holy Land.

There are many churches and ministries that offer tours of Israel. You can also take part in an archaeological dig or even take classes in Israel. See the addresses on the next page.

Tours and Archaeological Projects:

- BibleArchaeology.org
- MaranathaTours.com

Classes in Israel:

- IbexSemester.com
- JUC.edu
- Talbot.edu/academics/biblelands

Did You Know?

In his video lesson, Sean talked about the discovery of the Dead Sea Scrolls. Here are some facts about the Dead Sea Scrolls:

- They were discovered in 1947, shortly after World War II.

- There are more than nine hundred texts, including fragments of every book of the Bible except Esther.

- The scrolls date from 200 BC to AD 68 and were the library of a Jewish sect called the Essenes.

- The scrolls even include a treasure map of sorts. The Copper Scroll lists sixty-four hiding places throughout Israel that contain gold and silver. Most likely, these are the (still-undiscovered) treasures from the Jewish Temple that were hidden to keep them safe.

- In 1954, some of the scrolls were advertised for sale in *The Wall Street Journal*. The ad read, "The Four Dead Sea Scrolls: Biblical manuscripts dating back to at least 200 BC are for sale. This would be an ideal gift to an educational or religious institution by an individual or group. Box F206."

- When scholars compared the biblical texts in the Dead Sea Scrolls to our current Bible, they found textual differences of less than five percent. The majority of the differences are the equivalent of a "typo" in that they are slight spelling differences. There are no doctrinal differences, meaning that none of the differences significantly impact the meaning of the verse or cause us to change how we interpret the Scriptures.

The Dead Sea Scrolls are a very significant discovery because they give us insight into the culture of Israel in the first century—the time of Jesus' ministry and the writing of the New Testament. They also give us a high degree of confidence in the accuracy with which the Bible has been copied and passed down through time.

How do the facts regarding the Dead Sea Scrolls affect your view of the Bible? Explain your answer.

_____

_____

_____

_____

_____

_____

Has anyone you know ever challenged the accuracy of the Bible by saying that the text has been altered over time? How could you use the information about the Dead Sea Scrolls to answer that person?

_____

_____

_____

_____

_____

_____

_____

DAY 2

A key teaching in *GodQuest* is that what we believe directly affects our decisions. You can test this by thinking about what you would do in certain situations if you believed the Bible is the true and inspired Word of God and what you would do if you didn't believe that. For each situation below, look up and read the Bible verse(s); then fill in the columns.

SITUATION	RELEVANT BIBLE VERSE(S)
Your boyfriend (or girlfriend) wants to "move forward" in your relationship by having sex and moving in together. You think you might be falling in love with him (or her).	Ephesians 5:3 Colossians 3:5 1 Thessalonians 4:3–5
You go through a financial course at the new church you're attending, and the teacher encourages you to tithe (give 10 percent of your income to the church). Your budget is tight, and you're trying to buy a new car in the next few months.	Luke 16:13 Malachi 3:10 2 Corinthians 9:7
A teenage girl you know through your family becomes pregnant. She's an excellent student and planning to go to a good college. She is thinking about having an abortion, and she asks your advice.	Jeremiah 1:5 Psalm 139:13–16
A close friend is going through a difficult time, and you allow him to stay at your home for a while. Later, you realize your friend used your ATM card and PIN number to take money from your savings account.	Colossians 3:13 Matthew 6:14–15

IF I BELIEVED THE BIBLE IS TRUE, I WOULD ...	IF I DIDN'T BELIEVE THE BIBLE IS TRUE, I WOULD ...

GodQuest Profile: King David

He was the shepherd-king, the songwriter and musician, the mighty warrior God described as a "man after his own heart" (1 Samuel 13:14). Historians place David's reign at about 1000 BC. When the prophet Samuel carried out God's direction to anoint him as king, David was just a teenager, with "beautiful eyes and a handsome appearance" (1 Samuel 16:12 NASB). Throughout his life, David was a leader with unwavering faith and a courageous heart, but he was also a man who fell prey to temptation. He was inspiring, heroic, and oh so human.

Now, three thousand years separate us from Israel's famed King David. Some people believe King David is just a legendary character, no more real than King Arthur. But the Scriptures record the details of his life and writings in no fewer than six Old Testament books. Fact or fantasy—which is King David, and how can we know?

Tel Dan Stele

In 1993 and 1994, archaeologists working at Tel Dan, the remains of an ancient city in northern Israel, discovered two stone fragments that date to sometime between 841–798 BC. The fragments, referred to as the Tel Dan Stele, contain an inscription from an Aramaic king who brags of his military conquests: "I killed Joram son of Ahab king of Israel, and I killed Achazyahu son of Joram king of the House of David." The Tel Dan Stele is the first artifact known to reference King David.

When you're reading the Bible, the people in it can feel like characters in a story rather than real people. Why do you think that is?

_____

_____

_____

_____

_____

What could you do to better connect with King David and the other men and women whose lives are described in the Bible?

_____

_____

_____

_____

_____

_____

WANT MORE? If you would like more evidence for the life of King David, do an Internet search on "stepped stone structure City of David." It is a sixty-foot-high stone retaining wall dated to sometime between the later years of the twelfth century and the eleventh century BC. The structure functioned as a city wall and probably supported a large building. In 2005, a well-known archaeologist discovered a large, multiroom stone structure she dated to the time of David. The large structure rests atop the stepped wall, and many archaeologists believe the discovery could be the palace of King David.

They Said It

"*I know of no finding in archaeology that's properly confirmed which is in opposition to the Scriptures. The Bible is the most accurate history textbook the world has ever seen.*" —Dr. Clifford Wilson, former director of the Australian Institute of Archaeology

"*In regard to this Great Book, I have but to say, it is the best gift God has given to man. All the good the Savior gave to the world was communicated through this book. But for it we could not know right from wrong. All things most desirable for man's welfare, here and hereafter, are to be found portrayed in it.*" —Abraham Lincoln

"*In every instance where the findings of archaeology pertain to the Biblical record, the archaeological evidence confirms, sometimes in detailed fashion, the historical accuracy of Scripture. In those instances where the archaeological findings seem to be at variance with the Bible, the discrepancy lies with the archaeological evidence, i.e., improper interpretation, lack of evidence, etc.—not with the Bible.*" —Dr. Bryant C. Wood, archaeologist, Associates for Biblical Research

"*It is impossible to rightly govern the world without God and the Bible.*" —George Washington

"*There can be no doubt that archaeology has confirmed the substantial historicity of Old Testament tradition.*" —Dr. William F. Albright, archaeologist and Bible scholar

Have you ever watched a TV show, seen a movie, or read an article that challenged the authenticity and accuracy of the Bible? Did you experience any doubts? Did you do any additional investigation on the evidence presented?

_____

_____

_____

_____

_____

_____

In what ways has the Bible affected law and cultural practice in America? What about in other countries?

_____

_____

_____

_____

_____

_____

Reflections from Your Journey

As you think back over the video teaching, discussion questions, and *Travel Logs* from this week, what made the biggest impression on you? Why?

_____

_____

_____

_____

_____

_____

Was there anything that surprised you? What was it and why?

_____

_____

_____

_____

_____

_____

Go back to Starting Location Question 2 and look at your answers. After this week's lesson, would you change any of your answers? If so, why?

_____

_____

_____

_____

_____

In what ways would you like to increase your knowledge of the Bible and its impact on your life? List a few those goals below.

_____

_____

_____

_____

_____

Finish this week's study by spending some time in prayer. Praise God for revealing truth, His character, and His plans in the Bible. Ask Him to speak to you through His Word as you read the Bible this week. Share with Him your goals for this study, and pray for Him to help you achieve those goals.

Next Week: "The Question"

What you believe about God's goodness defines your relationship with Him.

"In this world you will have trouble. But take heart! I have overcome the world."

—John 16:33

SIGNPOST 4:

THE QUESTION

WHAT YOU BELIEVE ABOUT GOD'S GOODNESS DEFINES YOUR RELATIONSHIP WITH HIM.

If you could ask God any question and you knew He would answer you, what would you ask? The question most people want to ask God is, "Why do you allow so much pain and suffering?" We look around at the beauty of God's creation and we read about Jesus in the Bible, and our hearts tell us that God is good and fair. At the same time, every news program we watch and every newspaper we pick up makes us confront the fact that the world is full of tragic stories. Rebel soldiers wipe out a peaceful village. A child is kidnapped and murdered. A devastating tsunami hits a nation already struggling with poverty. Someone we love is diagnosed with cancer. There is terrible pain in the world. God is good. And God is all-powerful. How can all three of these statements be true?

In some cases, we make a wrong decision, and tough consequences result. In other situations, though, heartbreaking tragedy strikes kind, ethical, generous people, and it seems beyond explanation. There are moments when we want to cry out to God and simply ask, "Why?" At those times, we encounter a Signpost that reads, "What you believe about God's goodness defines your relationship with Him." We can choose to trust God even when we don't understand, or we can turn our backs on Him and walk away.

This week we're going to address "The Question": how can a good God allow pain and suffering?

Open your study with prayer.

Ask God to guide your thoughts and your words during your study. The Bible says God is a God of truth, so pray for Him to reveal truth as you watch the *GodQuest* video teaching, study the Bible, and answer this week's questions.

Starting Location

Use these first questions to find out *where you are* in your views on the Bible.

Icebreaker Question

Take a moment and think about some of the sad stories you have heard in the news or from the lives of people around you. Of those stories, which has touched you the most deeply? Which one was the most difficult to understand and accept? Why?

_____

_____

_____

TRAVEL TIP: For this specific question, choose something that happened in another person's life, not your own. In this week's *Travel Logs*, you will have an opportunity to reflect on the pain and trials in your own life.

QUESTION 1

During His ministry, Jesus said we would have trouble in this world, and there is certainly plenty of trouble on the news every night. Trouble does not exist as an abstract concept; we all experience it personally in some way or another. How anxious are you about having to face pain in your life? Look at each of the trials listed below and on the next page indicate how much you worry about that particular issue.

A serious medical issue (such as cancer)

___ Very worried ___ A little worried ___ Not at all worried

Losing your job

___ Very worried ___ A little worried ___ Not at all worried

A car or plane accident

__ Very worried __ A little worried __ Not at all worried

A natural disaster (such as an earthquake, tornado, or flood)

__ Very worried __ A little worried __ Not at all worried

A severe economic decline

__ Very worried __ A little worried __ Not at all worried

Loss of an important relationship (divorce or loss of a girlfriend/boyfriend)

__ Very worried __ A little worried __ Not at all worried

When you're done, share your answers with your group.

QUESTION 2

Below, indicate your level of agreement with each statement.

Most of the pain in the world is caused by people.

__ Strongly Agree __ Agree __ Uncertain __ Disagree __ Strongly Disagree

God is responsible for natural disasters like floods, earthquakes, tsunamis, and tornadoes.

__ Strongly Agree __ Agree __ Uncertain __ Disagree __ Strongly Disagree

There have been times in my life when I was angry at God.

__ Strongly Agree __ Agree __ Uncertain __ Disagree __ Strongly Disagree

God is good and fair.

__ Strongly Agree __ Agree __ Uncertain __ Disagree __ Strongly Disagree

When you're done, share your answers with your group.

TRAVEL TIP: As you listen to other people share their answers, remember that gentleness and respect are important characteristics for a good group discussion. Allow other group members to share without judging their answers or attempting to correct them.

Directions from Your Guides

Play the Signpost 4 video on your *GodQuest* Resource DVD.

After you watch the video lesson, answer the following questions. If you're doing *GodQuest* with a group, share your answers with the other group members.

QUESTION 3

In this week's video, Sean explained that we cry out against the injustice and evil of the world because we believe in goodness and justice. He also shared that C. S. Lewis realized that our cries for justice when we experience pain are clues that the universe was designed to be a just place created by a good God. What's your reaction to Sean's point?

_____

_____

_____

_____

QUESTION 4

Dave Dravecky talked about a choice we face during times of pain and suffering. We can turn away from God or turn toward Him for His grace and comfort. Have you faced a choice like this in your life? What happened, and how did you make your choice?

_____

_____

_____

_____

Trip Planner

READ: Genesis 3:1–19

"Cursed is the ground because of you; through painful toil you will eat of it all the days of your life. It will produce thorns and thistles for you, and you will eat the plants of the field. By the sweat of your brow you will eat your food until you return to the ground, since from it you were taken; for dust you are and to dust you will return." —Genesis 3:17–19

QUESTION 5

In Genesis 3:16–19 God tells Adam and Eve the consequences of their sin. In the chart below, write down one or more of the consequences given in each verse. Then see if you can think of an example of how each verse is true in our world. For example, in verse 17 God tells Adam that the ground is now "cursed." What do you think this means, and can you list some ways in which you think the earth itself shows the effects of sin?

VERSE	CONSEQUENCE(S)	EXAMPLE
16		
17	"Cursed is the ground because of you …"	
18		
19		

READ: Genesis 6:11–12, Proverbs 21:10, Matthew 24:12, Romans 1:28–32

Now the earth was corrupt in God's sight and was full of violence. God saw how corrupt the earth had become, for all the people on earth had corrupted their ways. —Genesis 6:11–12

The wicked man craves evil; his neighbor gets no mercy from him.
—Proverbs 21:10

Because of the increase of wickedness, the love of most will grow cold …
—Matthew 24:12

Furthermore, since they did not think it worthwhile to retain the knowledge of God, he gave them over to a depraved mind, to do what ought not to be done. They have become filled with every kind of wickedness, evil, greed and depravity. They are full of envy, murder, strife, deceit and malice. They are gossips, slanderers, God-haters, insolent, arrogant and boastful; they invent ways of doing evil; they disobey their parents; they are senseless, faithless, heartless, ruthless. Although they know God's righteous decree that those who do such things deserve death, they not only continue to do these very things but also approve of those who practice them. —Romans 1:28–32

QUESTION 6

As you consider the pain and suffering in this world, how much of it do you think is caused by people? How do the verses you just read explain this?

_____

_____

_____

_____

READ: Job 1:6–7, 2:1–2, 1 Peter 5:8

One day the angels came to present themselves before the LORD, and Satan also came with them. The LORD said to Satan, "Where have you come from?" Satan answered the LORD, "From roaming through the earth and going back and forth in it." —Job 1:6–7

On another day the angels came to present themselves before the LORD, and Satan also came with them to present himself before him. And the LORD said to Satan, "Where have you come from?" Satan answered the LORD, "From roaming through the earth and going back and forth in it." —Job 2:1–2

Be self-controlled and alert. Your enemy the devil prowls around like a roaring lion looking for someone to devour. —1 Peter 5:8

QUESTION 7

How do the previous passages explain some of the evil and pain in the world?

_____

_____

_____

_____

READ: Genesis 18:20–26, Psalms 9:8, 33:5

TRAVEL TIP: If you have time, read all of Genesis 18:20–33 so you have more insight into what happened between Abraham and God regarding the fate of Sodom.

"Far be it from you to do such a thing—to kill the righteous with the wicked, treating the righteous and the wicked alike. Far be it from you! Will not the Judge of all the earth do right?" —Genesis 18:25

He will judge the world in righteousness; he will govern the peoples with justice. —Psalm 9:8

The LORD loves righteousness and justice; the earth is full of his unfailing love. —Psalm 33:5

QUESTION 8

After reading all of these verses, how would you answer Abraham's question, "Will not the Judge of all the earth do right?" To what extent do you trust God to be fair and merciful? If you don't fully trust Him, what holds you back?

_____

_____

_____

READ: Genesis 50:20, Romans 8:28

"You intended to harm me, but God intended it for good to accomplish what is now being done, the saving of many lives." —Genesis 50:20

And we know that in all things God works for the good of those who love him, who have been called according to his purpose. —Romans 8:28

QUESTION 9

The Bible teaches us that God is not the source of evil and that He can use difficult, heartbreaking circumstances for good. Take a moment to think about some of the tough times in your life. Was there anything good that came out of those trials? Do you think a person's attitude affects whether God uses pain in their life for good? Why or why not?

_____

_____

_____

_____

READ: Isaiah 53:3, John 16:33, 2 Corinthians 1:3–4, Hebrews 4:15

MAP LEGEND:

Isaiah 53:3 is a prophecy written around 700 BC, and it describes Jesus. The "high priest" in Hebrews 4:15 is also a reference to Jesus.

He was despised and rejected by men, a man of sorrows, and familiar with suffering. Like one from whom men hide their faces he was despised, and we esteemed him not. —Isaiah 53:3

"In this world you will have trouble. But take heart! I have overcome the world." —John 16:33

Praise be to the God and Father of our Lord Jesus Christ, the Father of compassion and the God of all comfort, who comforts us in all our troubles, so that we can comfort those in any trouble with the comfort we ourselves have received from God. —2 Corinthians 1:3–4

For we do not have a high priest who is unable to sympathize with our weaknesses, but we have one who has been tempted in every way, just as we are—yet was without sin. —Hebrews 4:15

QUESTION 10

What comfort do you find in the previous verses? What do they tell you about God and His understanding of suffering?

_____

_____

_____

_____

QUESTION 11

Think of the examples Pastor Miles gave in the video—how did the two people he described "comfort others with the comfort [they themselves] have received from God?" How can you take what you've experienced in your own life and use it to comfort others?

_____

_____

_____

_____

Close your weekly study with prayer. If you're doing the *GodQuest* study in a group, ask group members to share prayer requests; then close your group meeting in prayer.

BEFORE NEXT WEEK'S STUDY, BE SURE TO COMPLETE *THE WEEKLY QUEST* AND THE DAILY *TRAVEL LOGS*.

If you would like to dig deeper into the topics from this week, read Signpost 4 in *GodQuest* by Sean McDowell and Stan Jantz.

The Weekly Quest

What touched you the most in this week's lesson? Is there a topic, a person, or a question that interests you the most? Below are some of the topics we covered this week, along with some suggested books, websites, and resources. Pick one or more topics and do a little research of your own. After you complete this week's *Travel Logs*, you might want to circle back to this section. The *Travel Logs* might arouse your curiosity about a specific topic.

SPECIAL CHALLENGE FOR THIS WEEK: READ THE BOOK OF JOB

The problem of pain and suffering is so difficult and so important that a whole book in the Bible is dedicated to the topic. This week (or over the next two weeks, if you're really busy), read the book of Job. It is the story of a righteous man who suffers enormous tragedy and loss. It can be a difficult book to read, particularly when God permits Satan to inflict pain on Job. At the same time, the book can teach you some profound and valuable lessons about suffering and about life. In the end, the comfort Job receives is the presence of God Himself. Job's trial and his example can help you understand and endure difficult times in your own life.

PERSONAL STORIES FROM PEOPLE WHO HAVE DEALT WITH GREAT PAIN OR DIFFICULTY

Dave Dravecky

One of the *GodQuest* guides for this week's video lesson, Dave Dravecky is a former major-league pitcher who lost his arm and shoulder to cancer.

Books:

- *Comeback*
- *When You Can't Come Back*
- *The Worth of a Man*
- *Called Up*

Websites:

- DaveDravecky.com

Steven Curtis Chapman and Mary Beth Chapman

Steven Curtis Chapman is a popular Christian musician. He and his wife, Mary Beth, lost their young daughter Maria in a tragic car accident, and they have used their experiences with their adopted daughters to minister to orphans worldwide.

Books:

- *Choosing to See* by Mary Beth Chapman, Steven Curtis Chapman, and Ellen Vaughn

Websites:

- StevenCurtisChapman.com
- MaryBethChapman.com
- ShowHope.org

Other Resources:

- You can find Steven Curtis Chapman's music at your local Christian bookstore or online.

Joni Eareckson Tada

Injured in a 1967 diving accident, Joni Eareckson Tada has become a well-known inspirational artist, speaker, and author.

Books:

- *Joni: An Unforgettable Story* by Joni Eareckson Tada and Billy Graham
- *Place of Healing* by Joni Eareckson Tada
- Many other books

Websites:

- JoniAndFriends.org
- JoniEarecksonTadaStory.com

Bethany Hamilton

Surfer Bethany Hamilton lost her arm to a shark attack at age thirteen but overcame the odds to become a professional surfer.

Books:

- *Soul Surfer* by Bethany Hamilton
- *Soul Surfer: Catching God's Wave for Your Life* by Jeremy and Janna Jones
- Many other books

Websites:

- BethanyHamilton.com
- SoulSurferWave.com
- SoulSurferTheMovie.com

Movies and Video Resources:

- *Soul Surfer*
- *Heart of a Soul Surfer*
- *SOUL SURFER* DVD-based Study

Nick Vujicic

Born without any limbs, Nick has become an inspirational author and speaker.

Books:

- *Life Without Limbs* by Nick Vujicic

Websites:

- LifeWithoutLimbs.org

Video Resources:

- *Verve*
- *Life's Greater Purpose*

GODQUEST

HEAVEN

In Revelation 21:4, the Bible tells us this about God and heaven: *"He will wipe every tear from their eyes. There will be no more death or mourning or crying or pain, for the old order of things has passed away."*

Read the Day 4 *Travel Log* on the topic of heaven. If you would like to read more about heaven, we recommend:

Books:

• *Heaven* by Randy Alcorn

• *Heaven Is for Real* by Todd Burpo with Lynn Vincent

• *Everything You Ever Wanted to Know about Heaven…but Never Dreamed of Asking* by Peter Kreeft

COMFORTING AND SERVING OTHERS

Books:

• *DO Something!* by Miles McPherson

• *The Hole in Our Gospel* by Richard Stearns

• *The Cause Within You* by Matthew Barnett with George Barna

Websites:

• DoSomethingWorld.org

• PutYourFaithInAction.org

• WorldVision.org

GOD'S COMFORT

Books:

• *Where Is God When It Hurts?* by Philip Yancey

• *The Problem of Pain* by C. S. Lewis

ANSWERING THE PROBLEM OF EVIL

Books:

• *If God, Why Evil?* by Norman Geisler

TRAVEL LOGS

DAY 1
The Suffering of Job

The Bible makes it clear that Job was a righteous man: *"In the land of Uz there lived a man whose name was Job. This man was blameless and upright; he feared God and shunned evil"* (Job 1:1). When God pointed out Job's righteousness to Satan, Satan claimed that Job was dedicated to God only because God had blessed him and protected him. In response, God permitted Satan to take away Job's wealth, health, and even all of his children. Job's response was to say, *"Naked I came from my mother's womb, and naked I will depart. The LORD gave and the LORD has taken away; may the name of the LORD be praised"* (Job 1:21). Three of Job's friends arrived, but rather than simply comforting him, they claimed that Job had brought the suffering on himself through his sin. Even as Job grieved for his children, suffered through poverty and physical pain, and stood up to his friends' questioning, he continued to hold on to his faith and remained true to God.

As you read through Job this week, consider some of the key lessons:

- Bad things happen, even to good people (Job 31, 42:7–8).
- All of creation belongs to God, and He can do as He chooses (Job 40).
- God protects his people (Job 1:10).
- God is our comforter, and one way He comforts us is with His presence (Job 42).
- God understands all things, and our own understanding is limited (Job 38–42).

Job trusted God and continued to praise Him even in the midst of great pain and tragedy. How do you think Job's response affected the people around him?

Job lived several thousand years ago. How many people do you think have heard or read his story? How much of an impact do you think his story and his example have had on the world?

_____

_____

_____

_____

_____

_____

_____

_____

_____

_____

_____

_____

_____

_____

_____

_____

_____

THE BOOK OF JOB

CHAPTER I

THERE was a man *b*in the land of Uz, whose name was *d*Job; and that man was *e*perfect and upright, and one that *f*feared God, and eschewed evil.

2 And there were born unto him seven sons and three daugh-

10 *a*Hast not thou made an hedge about him, and about his house, and about all that he hath on every side? *c*thou hast blessed the work of his hands, and his ¹substance is increased in the land.

11 *g*But put forth thine hand now, and touch all that he hath, ²and he will *h*curse thee to thy face.

12 And the LORD said unto Satan, Behold, all that he hath is in thy ⁴power; only upon him

a Ps. 34. 7
Is. 5. 2

b 1 Chr. 1. 17
c Ps. 128. 1, 2
Prov. 10. 22
d Ezek. 14. 14
Jas. 5. 11
e Gen. 17. 1
1 Or, cattle
f Prov. 16. 6
g ch. 2. 5
& 19. 21
2 Heb. if he
curse thee not
to thy face
h Is. 8. 21
Mal. 3. 13, 14

DAY 2

The Apostle Paul had a very-experienced perspective on the suffering we endure in this life. As a follower of Jesus Christ, he endured torture, prison, hunger, and constant danger (read 2 Corinthians 11:22–27 for Paul's description of his sufferings). Just before his execution, Paul wrote from a Roman prison to his protégé, Timothy. In this last letter, Paul summarized his life:

> For I am already being poured out like a drink offering, and the time has come for my departure. I have fought the good fight, I have finished the race, I have kept the faith. Now there is in store for me the crown of righteousness, which the Lord, the righteous Judge, will award to me on that day—and not only to me, but also to all who have longed for his appearing. —2 Timothy 4:6–8

In an earlier letter to Christians in the Greek city of Philippi, Paul compared the promise of heaven to life on earth. Read what Paul had to say:

> For to me, to live is Christ and to die is gain. If I am to go on living in the body, this will mean fruitful labor for me. Yet what shall I choose? I do not know! I am torn between the two: I desire to depart and be with Christ, which is better by far; but it is more necessary for you that I remain in the body. Convinced of this, I know that I will remain. —Philippians 1:21–25

In 2 Timothy, Paul refers to his life as an offering. In Philippians, he talks about using his life to labor for God. The concept in these Bible passages is that we are to live *for* God. How is that a foreign idea in our self-centered world?

_____

_____

_____

_____

_____

_____

_____

What do you think about the idea of living for God and having your life be an offering to Him? Have you ever considered that concept?

_____

_____

_____

_____

_____

_____

_____

_____

If you were to completely live for God, how would you want your life to affect the world around you? What would have to change for you to do that? How do you think God could use that offering?

_____

_____

_____

_____

_____

_____

_____

_____

_____

GodQuest Profile: Horatio Spafford

In 1873, a man named Horatio Spafford wrote a beautiful, inspiring song he titled "It Is Well with My Soul." If you just read the title and the chorus of the song, you might think Horatio Spafford's life was going well. Not so. In 1871, Spafford was unfortunate enough to lose his life savings in the great Chicago fire. Two years later, he had recovered to the point that he was going on a vacation to England with his wife and four daughters. Horatio had to stay a few extra days in the U.S., so he sent his family on ahead, planning to join them later. On November 22, 1873, while the Spafford family was crossing the Atlantic, their ship struck another vessel, and 226 people died. Horatio's wife survived, but all four of his daughters lost their lives in the tragic accident. Horatio boarded a ship for England, planning to reunite with his wife. It was while he was on board the ship, near the area where his young daughters had perished, that Spafford wrote "It Is Well with My Soul."

Take some time to read and consider a few of the verses of the song below. You can also hear the song by doing a search on YouTube. At least one version on YouTube includes pictures of Spafford and his family.

When peace, like a river, attendeth my way,
When sorrows like sea billows roll;
Whatever my lot, Thou has taught me to say,
It is well, it is well, with my soul.

Chorus:

It is well, with my soul,
It is well, it is well, with my soul.

And Lord, haste the day when my faith shall be sight,
The clouds be rolled back as a scroll;
The trump shall resound, and the Lord shall descend,
Even so, it is well with my soul.

Use the space below to write your reaction to the song and to Horatio Spafford's attitude toward his personal tragedy.

Heaven

Suppose you wake up one morning and the water heater isn't working; you have to take a freezing cold shower. Then you step on something slippery in your bare feet and realize your dog has thrown up on the floor. When you try to make your breakfast, the power shorts out, and you have to leave without eating. As you're driving to work, someone runs a red light and smashes the right side of your car—without having insurance. You show up late to work, so your boss fires you. When you get home, there's a notice from the bank, and you realize someone stole your ATM number and cleaned out your account.

The next day, you get a phone call offering you the job of your dreams at three times the pay you had before. The next phone call is from that big contest you entered—you just won five million dollars! You go to get the mail, and there's a notice that you've won an all-expenses-paid Mediterranean cruise. And every day afterward is just as great.

Right before you died, if someone asked you if you had a good life, what would you say? Would you tell them about that one bad day? Probably not, right?

Now think about your life on earth as just a part of a life that extends into eternity. The Bible tells us this about heaven: "*No eye has seen, no ear has heard, no mind has conceived what God has prepared for those who love him* …" (1 Corinthians 2:9).

Mother Teresa once said, "In light of Heaven, the worst suffering on earth, a life full of the most atrocious tortures on earth, will be seen to be no more serious than one night in an inconvenient hotel."

Have you ever thought about your life in the context of eternity? How does looking forward to heaven affect your view of pain and suffering in this life?

_____

_____

_____

_____

_____

_____

_____

_____

_____

_____

_____

_____

_____

Reflections from Your Journey

As you think back over the video teaching, discussion questions, and *Travel Logs* from this week, what made the biggest impression on you? Why?

_____

_____

_____

READ: Romans 5:3–5, James 1:2–4

"We also rejoice in our sufferings, because we know that suffering produces perseverance; perseverance, character; and character, hope. And hope does not disappoint us …" —Romans 5:3–5

"Consider it pure joy, my brothers, whenever you face trials of many kinds, because you know that the testing of your faith develops perseverance. Perseverance must finish its work so that you may be mature and complete, not lacking anything." —James 1:2–4

Fill in the table below, listing two or three of the most difficult times in your life. Write down a short description of what happened. In the second column, write down the hardest, most painful part of that trial. Finally, if something good came out of that experience or if you learned anything, write that down as well.

DIFFICULT TIME IN MY LIFE	HARDEST, MOST PAINFUL PART	SOMETHING GOOD OR SOMETHING I LEARNED

As you look over your answers, think about the teaching in James 1:2–4. How does your experience match up with the Bible passage?

_____

_____

_____

_____

Were you able to read the book of Job this week? What did you learn from Job's suffering, his reaction, and his conclusions? How can you apply those lessons to your own life?

_____

_____

_____

_____

Finish this week's study by spending some time in prayer. Praise God for His wisdom, His understanding of the future, and His perfect plan. If you are in the midst of pain or difficulty, ask God to guide you and to bring you His comfort. Pray for God to show you how you can live for Him and how you can comfort others who are suffering.

Next Week: "The King"

What you believe about Jesus' identity determines your path in life.

On his robe and
on his thigh he has this
name written:
KING OF KINGS AND LORD OF LORDS.

—Revelation 19:16

GODQUEST

SIGNPOST 5:
THE KING
WHAT YOU BELIEVE ABOUT JESUS' IDENTITY DETERMINES YOUR PATH IN LIFE.

When He was more than halfway through His earthly ministry, Jesus asked His twelve disciples a critical question. They were in Caesarea Philippi, in the far northern region of Israel, and the disciples had already seen their master and teacher calm a storm, feed five thousand people, walk on water, and heal the blind. After teaching them, living with them, and enabling them to witness miracles, Jesus asked the twelve men closest to Him two questions to help them make sense of it all.

First, He asked them, *"Who do people say the Son of Man is?" They replied, "Some say John the Baptist; others say Elijah; and still others, Jeremiah or one of the prophets"* (Matthew 16:13–14). Then Jesus upped the intensity of the discussion by asking them an all-important, very personal question: *"But what about you?" he asked. "Who do you say I am?" Simon Peter answered, "You are the Christ, the Son of the living God." Jesus replied, "Blessed are you, Simon son of Jonah, for this was not revealed to you by man, but by my Father in heaven"* (Matthew 16:15–17).

Few would dispute that Jesus had a more dramatic impact on our world than anyone who has ever lived. It has been more than two thousand years since He walked this earth, yet Jesus is still a key figure in every major world religion. So who is Jesus really? In this week's video lesson, you'll see people answer that question, and you'll hear a wide range of responses: a prophet, a good man, a myth, a religious leader, the Son of God. But the important question is the one you have to answer on your own at the end of the lesson: who do *you* say Jesus is?

As you go through this lesson to prepare to answer that question, you will encounter Signpost 5, which says that what you believe about Jesus' identity determines your path in life. You can either follow Jesus or trek out on your own. Which path will you follow?

GUIDEBOOK

105

Open your study with prayer.

Ask God to guide your thoughts and your words during your study. The Bible says God is a God of truth, so pray for Him to reveal truth as you watch the *GodQuest* video teaching, study the Bible, and answer this week's questions.

Starting Location

Use these first questions to find out *where you are* in your views on the Bible.

Icebreaker Question

The way people see us is not always who we really are. So who do you say *you* are? Answer this question by describing to your group how you see yourself and then describing how you think other people see you. For example, someone might answer by saying, "I am a follower of Jesus and then a mother and wife. But people at work might see me more as a leader because I have to be one there."

_____

_____

If your two descriptions (how you see yourself and how others see you) differ, why do you think the discrepancy exists?

_____

_____

_____

QUESTION 1

Throughout history, people have used a lot of adjectives to describe Jesus. Read through this list and choose the three words that best describe how you view Jesus:

___ Holy	___ Humble	___ Loving	___ Gracious
___ Powerful	___ Angry	___ Brave	___ Accepting
___ Judgmental	___ Wise	___ Compassionate	___ Servant
___ Just	___ Protective	___ Other _____

When you're done, share your answers with your group.

QUESTION 2

Indicate your level of agreement with the following statements:

I have read the four Gospels and am familiar with Jesus' life and ministry.

__ Strongly Agree __ Agree __ Uncertain __ Disagree __ Strongly Disagree

Most of what I know about Jesus, I've learned from other people.

__ Strongly Agree __ Agree __ Uncertain __ Disagree __ Strongly Disagree

During His ministry, Jesus claimed to be God.

__ Strongly Agree __ Agree __ Uncertain __ Disagree __ Strongly Disagree

I have read books or articles or watched TV shows that have caused me to question Jesus' identity (who He really is).

__ Strongly Agree __ Agree __ Uncertain __ Disagree __ Strongly Disagree

Jesus' life has been accurately recorded in the Bible.

__ Strongly Agree __ Agree __ Uncertain __ Disagree __ Strongly Disagree

When you're done, share your answers with your group.

TRAVEL TIP: As you listen to others share their answers, remember that gentleness and respect are important characteristics for a good group discussion. Allow other group members to share without judging their answers or attempting to correct them.

Directions from Your Guides

Play the Signpost 5 video on your *GodQuest* Resource DVD.

After you watch the video lesson, answer the following questions. If you're doing *GodQuest* with a group, share your answers with the other group members.

QUESTION 3

In this week's video, people gave a variety of answers to the question, Who was Jesus? Why do you think there are so many different views?

_____

_____

_____

_____

QUESTION 4

Sean talked about the fact that Jesus specifically claimed to be God. Before watching this week's video lesson, was that clear to you? If a friend, neighbor, or family member were to say that Jesus was just a good man and a religious teacher, would you know how to respond to that person? What would you say?

_____

_____

_____

QUESTION 5

As you listened to Dr. Strauss, which of his points made the biggest impression on you? Why?

_____

_____

_____

GODQUEST

Trip Planner

During this week's video lesson, Sean quoted C. S. Lewis' popular argument for the deity of Jesus:

"I am trying here to prevent anyone saying the really foolish thing that people often say about Him: I'm ready to accept Jesus as a great moral teacher, but I don't accept his claim to be God. That is the one thing we must not say. A man who was merely a man and said the sort of things Jesus said would not be a great moral teacher. He would either be a lunatic—on the level with the man who says he is a poached egg—or else he would be the Devil of Hell. You must make your choice. Either this man was, and is, the Son of God, or else a madman or something worse. You can shut him up for a fool, you can spit at him and kill him as a demon or you can fall at his feet and call him Lord and God, but let us not come with any patronising nonsense about his being a great human teacher. He has not left that open to us. He did not intend to.[1]

In this week's *Trip Planner*, we'll answer these questions:

1. Who did Jesus say He is?

2. Did He actually back up His claims?

READ: Exodus 3:14, John 8:56–59

God said to Moses, "I AM WHO I AM. This is what you are to say to the Israelites: 'I AM has sent me to you.'" —Exodus 3:14

"Your father Abraham rejoiced at the thought of seeing my day; he saw it and was glad." "You are not yet fifty years old," the Jews said to him, "and you have seen Abraham!" "I tell you the truth," Jesus answered, "before Abraham was born, I am!" At this, they picked up stones to stone him, but Jesus hid himself, slipping away from the temple grounds. —John 8:56–59

[1] C. S. Lewis, *Mere Christianity* (San Francisco: HarperCollins, 1952), 52.

The Hebrew word for *I* AM in Exodus 3:14 is related to the Hebrew word for *Lord* in 3:15 (YHWH). Bible scholars believe YHWH was pronounced "Yahweh." It was the Israelites' name for God, and they had such awe for God's holiness that they wouldn't even say this name out loud. Instead of using "YHWH," the Israelites would say "Adonai," which means "Lord."

QUESTION 6

Jesus was in Jerusalem speaking to the Jewish people and the religious leaders when he said the words in the previous verses. As part of Jesus' conversation with the religious leaders, He made a unique claim the Jews found outrageous. What's so astounding about Jesus' statement in John 8:58? How did the Jews react, and why do you think they were so angry?

_____

_____

_____

_____

READ: Matthew 11:27, John 10:24–33

"All things have been committed to me by my Father. No one knows the Son except the Father, and no one knows the Father except the Son and those to whom the Son chooses to reveal him." —Matthew 11:27

The Jews gathered around him, saying, "How long will you keep us in suspense? If you are the Christ, tell us plainly." Jesus answered, "I did tell you, but you do not believe. The miracles I do in my Father's name speak for me …" —John 10:24–25

"I and the Father are one." Again the Jews picked up stones to stone him, but Jesus said to them, "I have shown you many great miracles from the Father. For which of these do you stone me?" "We are not stoning you for any of these," replied the Jews, "but for blasphemy, because you, a mere man, claim to be God." —John 10:30–33

QUESTION 7

Think about C. S. Lewis' argument and then relate it to John 10:30–33. Based on their reaction, were the Jews clear about what Jesus was saying?

_____

_____

_____

READ: Mark 10:33–34, John 8:28

"We are going up to Jerusalem," he said, "and the Son of Man will be betrayed to the chief priests and teachers of the law. They will condemn him to death and will hand him over to the Gentiles, who will mock him and spit on him, flog him and kill him. Three days later he will rise." —Mark 10:33–34

So Jesus said, "When you have lifted up the Son of Man, then you will know that I am the one I claim to be and that I do nothing on my own but speak just what the Father has taught me." —John 8:28

QUESTION 8

In John 10:25, Jesus said, *"The miracles I do in my Father's name speak for me."* There was one incredible miracle that Jesus predicted in advance. What did Jesus mean when He said He would be *"lifted up"* (v. 28)? How do these two verses affect your confidence in Jesus' identity? How can you use them to answer skeptics?

_____

_____

READ: 1 Corinthians 15:3–6

For what I received I passed on to you as of first importance: that Christ died for our sins according to the Scriptures, that he was buried, that he was raised on the third day according to the Scriptures, and that he appeared to Peter, and then to the Twelve. After that, he appeared to more than five hundred of the brothers at the same time, most of whom are still living, though some have fallen asleep. —1 Corinthians 15:3–6

In the previous passage, how many people does the Apostle Paul claim saw Jesus after His resurrection? Paul wrote 1 Corinthians in approximately AD 55, a little more than twenty years after Jesus' crucifixion and resurrection. Most of the people who saw Jesus (during His ministry or after His resurrection) were, as Paul points out, still living at the time of his writing. If Paul or the other apostles had lied about Jesus' resurrection or had simply been misinformed, what might have happened?

_____

_____

_____

_____

READ: Luke 9:23–24

Then he said to them all: "If anyone would come after me, he must deny himself and take up his cross daily and follow me. For whoever wants to save his life will lose it, but whoever loses his life for me will save it." —Luke 9:23–24

QUESTION 10

During His ministry Jesus made many challenging and even counterintuitive statements. The passage in Luke 9:23–24 is a good example. Relate Jesus' words to your own life. Choose one or more of the phrases below and write down ways in which you:

Come after Jesus

Deny yourself

Take up your cross daily

Follow Jesus

Try to save your life

Lose your life for Jesus

Close your weekly study with prayer. If you're doing the *GodQuest* study in a group, ask group members to share prayer requests; then close your group meeting in prayer.

BEFORE NEXT WEEK'S STUDY, BE SURE TO COMPLETE *THE WEEKLY QUEST* AND THE DAILY *TRAVEL LOGS*.

If you would like to dig deeper into the topics from this week, read Signpost 5 in the GodQuest nonfiction book by Sean McDowell and Stan Jantz.

The Weekly Quest

The lists that follow include some of the topics we covered this week, along with suggested books, websites, and resources. Pick one or more topics and do a little research of your own. After you complete this week's *Travel Logs*, you might want to circle back to this section. The *Travel Logs* might arouse your curiosity about a specific topic.

CHRISTIANITY AND JESUS' IDENTITY

Books:

- *More Than a Carpenter* by Josh McDowell and Sean McDowell
- *The Case for Christ* by Lee Strobel
- *Four Portraits, One Jesus* by Mark L. Strauss

Websites:

- Josh.org
- SeanMcDowell.org
- LeeStrobel.com
- 4Truth.net

Videos:

- *The Passion of the Christ*
- *Jesus* (see JesusFilm.org)
- *The Case for Christ DVD* by Lee Strobel

JESUS' RESURRECTION

Books:

- *Evidence for the Resurrection* by John McDowell and Sean McDowell
- *The Case for the Resurrection of Jesus* by Gary R. Habermas and Michael Licona
- *The Resurrection of Jesus: A New Historiographical Approach* by Michael Licona

Websites:

- ReasonableFaith.org
- 4Truth.net

HISTORICAL EVIDENCE FOR THE LIFE OF JESUS

Books:

- *The Historical Jesus: Ancient Evidence for the Life of Christ* by Gary R. Habermas
- *Studying the Historical Jesus: A Guide to Sources and Methods* by Darrell L. Bock

ISRAEL DURING THE TIME OF JESUS

Websites:

- BiblePlaces.com

DAY 1

It was about this time that King Herod arrested some who belonged to the church, intending to persecute them. He had James, the brother of John, put to death with the sword. —Acts 12:1–2

Did You Know?

When the eleven remaining apostles and other early leaders of the Christian church began to proclaim the truth about Jesus, they were greatly persecuted by the Jewish religious leaders and the Romans. Most were imprisoned and beaten, and eventually almost all of them were martyred for their beliefs. While the Bible gives details only about the death of James, we have *tradition*—information passed down from the first- and second-century church leaders—regarding the deaths of these Christian leaders. The chart that follows lists the apostles and key leaders of the church and how each of them is understood to have died.

NAME	MANNER OF DEATH	NAME	MANNER OF DEATH
Peter	Crucified	Thomas	Stabbed by a lance
Andrew	Whipped and crucified	James (brother of Jesus)	Thrown from the Temple and then clubbed to death
James	Beheaded	Simon	Crucified
Philip	Crucified	John	Boiled in oil, but survived and died of nature causes
Bartholomew (also called Nathanael)	Whipped and crucified	Jude (also called Thaddaeus)	Crucified
Matthias	Stoned and then beheaded	Matthew	Killed by a sword
Paul	Beheaded		

All of these men knew Jesus personally (Jesus appeared to Paul after His resurrection), and most were witnesses to His crucifixion. Yet they all died for saying that Jesus rose from the dead and is the Son of God. Although many people have died for their religious *beliefs*, these men are unique in that they were in a position to *know* what was true.

What is your reaction to the apostles' willingness to be tortured and killed for maintaining that Jesus rose?

_____

_____

_____

_____

_____

_____

How does this impact your faith and your confidence in the testimony of the Gospels?

_____

_____

_____

_____

_____

_____

They Said It

"Alexander, Caesar, Charlemagne, and I have
founded empires. But on what did we rest the creations
of our genius? Upon force. Jesus Christ founded his
empire upon love, and at this hour millions of men
would die for him." —Napoleon Bonaparte

"Nero fastened the guilt and inflicted the most
exquisite tortures on a class hated for their
abominations, called Christians by the populace. Christus, from whom the
name had its origin, suffered the extreme penalty during the reign of Tiberius
at the hands of one of our procurators, Pontius Pilatus ..." —Tacitus, a first-
century Roman senator and historian, referring to Jesus' death at the hands of
Pontius Pilate.

"A man who was completely innocent offered himself as a sacrifice for the good
of others, including his enemies, and became the ransom of the world. It was a
perfect act." —Mahatma Gandhi

"I am an historian, I am not a believer, but I must confess as a historian that
this penniless preacher from Nazareth is irrevocably the very center of history.
Jesus Christ is easily the most dominant figure in all history." —H. G. Wells

"They (the Christians) were in the habit of meeting on a certain fixed day before
it was light, when they sang in alternate verses a hymn to Christ, as to a god ..."
—Pliny the Younger, a Roman governor, writing around AD 112 to Emperor
Trajan and describing the early Christians

"As a child I received instruction both in the Bible and in the Talmud. I am a
Jew, but I am enthralled by the luminous figure of the Nazarene. ... No one can
read the Gospels without feeling the actual presence of Jesus. His personality
pulsates in every word. No myth is filled with such life." —Albert Einstein

Which of these quotes affects you the most? Why?

_____

_____

_____

_____

_____

_____

_____

What do you hear people around you and in the media say about Jesus? How do their comments affect your own views?

_____

_____

_____

_____

_____

_____

_____

_____

When they came to the place called the Skull, there they crucified him, along with the criminals—one on his right, the other on his left. —Luke 23:33

Did You Know?

In 1968, in the midst of a construction project in Jerusalem, workers discovered the remains of a Jewish burial site containing thirty-five individual remains. The burial site was dated to approximately AD 70, during the time of Roman rule. The human remains were found in fifteen *ossuaries*—stone burial containers used during the time of Christ. The burial custom of the time was to place a body in a tomb, wait until the body had decomposed, and then move the bones to an ossuary.

One of the human skeletons was particularly interesting to religious scholars because the man, named Yohanan Ben Ha'galgol, had been crucified. A large nail, six to seven inches long, was still embedded in his feet, having been driven sideways through the heel bones. Scientists who examined the skeleton also found that nails had been driven through the lower section of the radius and ulna bones, near the wrists. The radius bones showed signs of repeated friction from the bone rubbing against the large nail. The friction could have been caused by Yohanan repeatedly pulling himself upward to breathe and then sinking back down into a lower position.

In addition, Yohanan's lower leg bones were broken from a single blow, most likely administered by a Roman solider. It was common for Roman soldiers to break the legs of crucifixion victims; doing so made it more difficult for the person to push upward to breathe and thus hastened the victim's death.

Compare this description of Yohanan's remains to the description the Apostle John gives of Jesus' crucifixion:

> *Because the Jews did not want the bodies left on the crosses during the Sabbath, they asked Pilate to have the legs broken and the bodies taken down. The soldiers therefore came and broke the legs of the first man who had been crucified with Jesus, and then those of the other. But when they came to Jesus and found that he was already dead, they did not break his legs.* —John 19:31–33

Toward the end of His ministry, Jesus deliberately journeyed toward Jerusalem, knowing the death that awaited Him. Take a few moments and think about Jesus' character and actions. Then, in the space provided, write a few sentences describing Him and His attitude about enduring crucifixion.

> *For God so loved the world that he gave his one and only Son, that whoever believes in him shall not perish but have eternal life.* —John 3:16

Write a short prayer to God telling Him your feelings about His love and sacrifice.

_____

_____

_____

_____

_____

_____

_____

_____

_____

_____

_____

_____

_____

_____

_____

_____

_____

DAY 4

READ: Matthew 4:19, John 12:26, Luke 9:23–24

"Come, follow me," Jesus said, "and I will make you fishers of men." —Matthew 4:19

"Whoever serves me must follow me; and where I am, my servant also will be. My Father will honor the one who serves me." —John 12:26

Then he said to them all: "If anyone would come after me, he must deny himself and take up his cross daily and follow me. For whoever wants to save his life will lose it, but whoever loses his life for me will save it." —Luke 9:23–24

"Follow me!" If you scan through the New Testament, you'll read this phrase (and invitation) from Jesus twenty times. It's an intriguing phrase to think about. What would it be like to actually follow the Son of God?

How would you say you have responded to Jesus' invitation? Evaluate your life using the following list. Next to each line, write what percentage of your time is spent following each person, group of people, or goal. For example, if you follow Jesus 30 percent of the time, write "30%" next to "Jesus." If you follow career goals 50 percent of the time, write "50%" next to "Career goals," and so on, until the numbers add up to 100 percent. You can assign 0 percent to a line that doesn't apply to you.

Percent of Time You Follow

____ Jesus

____ The example and advice of your friends

____ The pursuit of money

____ Your spouse or boyfriend/girlfriend

____ Career goals

____ Cultural examples (doing what's expected of you or what you see others doing)

____ Political leaders

____ Direction and advice from your parents

____ A religious leader other than Jesus

____ Other _____

[2] There are twenty mentions of "Follow me" in the New International Version of the New Testament Gospels.

As you look over your completed list, what can you conclude?

Is there anything you would like to change? If so, how could you make that change in your life?

Reflections from Your Journey

As you think back over the video teaching, discussion questions, and *Travel Logs* from this week, what made the biggest impression on you? Why?

_____

_____

_____

_____

Think about the two questions Jesus asked His own disciples. The first question was, "Who do people say I am?" If you asked your family and your closest friends (the people you spend the most time with) who Jesus is, how would they answer?

_____

_____

_____

_____

Now broaden the audience to the country where you live. What would most people there say about Jesus?

_____

_____

_____

_____

Now answer Jesus' most important question. Who do you say Jesus is? If you had to stand before a roomful of your friends, neighbors, and co-workers, what would you say about Jesus? Write your answer in the space provided.

_____

_____

_____

How confident are you of your answer? What would it take to make you even more confident, and how can you make that happen?

_____

_____

_____

Finish this week's study by spending some time in prayer. Lay before God any doubts you have. Commit to reading about Jesus in the four Gospels: Matthew, Mark, Luke, and John. Ask Jesus to reveal Himself to you as you read His Word and as you do any additional research.

If you don't have a relationship with Jesus Christ, talk with your small group leader about how to invite Jesus into your life. If you're doing this study with a group, talk with a pastor or a friend you know who follows Jesus.

Next Week: "The Path"

The path you follow in your spiritual journey determines your destination.

Jesus answered,
"I am the way and the truth
and the life. No one comes to the
Father except through me."

—John 14:6

SIGNPOST 6:
THE PATH
THE PATH YOU FOLLOW IN YOUR SPIRITUAL JOURNEY DETERMINES YOUR DESTINATION.

Three of the four Gospels include the story of when the disciple Levi (also called Matthew) first met Jesus. When the event occurred, Jesus was just beginning His earthly ministry and was teaching in the area of Galilee in the northern part of Israel. Luke tells the story this way: *After this, Jesus went out and saw a tax collector by the name of Levi sitting at his tax booth. "Follow me," Jesus said to him, and Levi got up, left everything and followed him* (Luke 5:27–28). What would cause a wealthy man to just get up, leave everything, and follow someone? There had to have been something about Jesus that caused Levi to know immediately that following Jesus was worth everything. Maybe he sensed the truth that Jesus later shared with His disciples: *"I am the way and the truth and the life. No one comes to the Father except through me"* (John 14:6).

Jesus made many radical statements during His ministry, and the one recorded in John 14:6 was one of the boldest … and most important. While thousands of people came to see Jesus, to watch Him perform miracles, and to hear His teaching, there were many who were angered and threatened by His claims—that He was the very Son of God and the only means of salvation.

Jesus once invited a tax collector to come follow Him, and He extends the same invitation to all of us. Levi dropped everything and made Jesus the only path he would follow for the rest of his life.

On this last week of *GodQuest*, we will encounter Signpost 6, which says that the path you follow in your spiritual journey determines your destination. Jesus said He is the one and only way to God and to heaven. Other people believe there are many paths to God. Which path are *you* on?

Open your study with prayer.

Ask God to guide your thoughts and your words during your study. The Bible says God is a God of truth, so pray for Him to reveal truth as you watch the *GodQuest* video teaching, study the Bible, and answer this week's questions.

Starting Location

Use these first questions to find out *where you are* in your views on the Bible.

Icebreaker Question

This week's study is about the paths we take and the decisions we make in life. Think of a difficult decision you once had to make. What choices did you have, and how did you arrive at your decision? Share your answer with the group.

QUESTION 1

In our culture, it's not politically correct to say Jesus and Christianity are the only way to God. Would you feel comfortable telling other people that Jesus is the only way to heaven? Why or why not?

GODQUEST

QUESTION 2

Indicate your level of agreement with the following statements:

If people do enough good deeds, they deserve to go to heaven.

___ Strongly Agree ___ Agree ___ Uncertain ___ Disagree ___ Strongly Disagree

There is some truth in all religions.

___ Strongly Agree ___ Agree ___ Uncertain ___ Disagree ___ Strongly Disagree

I'm familiar with the basic teachings of most major religions.

___ Strongly Agree ___ Agree ___ Uncertain ___ Disagree ___ Strongly Disagree

Mormons, Muslims, and Christians all worship the same God.

___ Strongly Agree ___ Agree ___ Uncertain ___ Disagree ___ Strongly Disagree

All people will eventually be saved because God loves us.

___ Strongly Agree ___ Agree ___ Uncertain ___ Disagree ___ Strongly Disagree

When you're done, share your answers with your group.

TRAVEL TIP: As you listen to others share their answers, remember that gentleness and respect are important characteristics for a good group discussion. Allow group members to share without judging their answers or attempting to correct them.

Directions from Your Guides

After you watch the video lesson, answer the following questions. If you're doing *GodQuest* with a group, share your answers with the other group members.

QUESTION 3

In this week's video, Greg Koukl says that all of us have a problem and that problem is sin. Even if you had never read or heard about how sin affects our relationship with God, would you have sensed that problem? Do you agree with Greg—that sin separates us from God? Why or why not?

_____

_____

_____

_____

QUESTION 4

What stood out to you most in Sean's teaching? Why?

_____

_____

_____

_____

Trip Planner

READ: Mark 7:21–23, Romans 3:23, Romans 6:23

"For from within, out of men's hearts, come evil thoughts, sexual immorality, theft, murder, adultery, greed, malice, deceit, lewdness, envy, slander, arrogance and folly. All these evils come from inside and make a man 'unclean.'"
—Mark 7:21–23

For all have sinned and fall short of the glory of God. —Romans 3:23

For the wages of sin is death, but the gift of God is eternal life in Christ Jesus our Lord. —Romans 6:23

QUESTION 5

What would you say is the human standard for deciding who should go to heaven? In other words, how do you think people would determine who is good enough to go to heaven?

_____

_____

_____

_____

Now summarize what these three Bible passages say about us earning our way to heaven. How would you describe God's standard for earning an eternity in heaven?

_____

_____

_____

READ: Romans 7:18–25

I know that nothing good lives in me, that is, in my sinful nature. For I have the desire to do what is good, but I cannot carry it out. For what I do is not the good I want to do; no, the evil I do not want to do—this I keep on doing. Now if I do what I do not want to do, it is no longer I who do it, but it is sin living in me that does it. So I find this law at work: When I want to do good, evil is right there with me. For in my inner being I delight in God's law; but I see another law at work in the members of my body, waging war against the law of my mind and making me a prisoner of the law of sin at work within my members. What a wretched man I am! Who will rescue me from this body of death? Thanks be to God—through Jesus Christ our Lord! So then, I myself in my mind am a slave to God's law, but in the sinful nature a slave to the law of sin. —Romans 7:18–25

QUESTION 6

Sean talked about putting a microphone inside a person's mind to hear the person's inner thoughts. How would you feel about going through that test? In what ways do you identify with Paul in Romans 7:18–25? What does Paul say is the solution to the problem of sin?

_____

_____

_____

_____

READ: 1 Corinthians 15:1–4

Now, brothers, I want to remind you of the gospel I preached to you, which you received and on which you have taken your stand. By this gospel you are saved, if you hold firmly to the word I preached to you. Otherwise, you have believed in vain. For what I received I passed on to you as of first importance: that Christ died for our sins according to the Scriptures, that he was buried, that he was raised on the third day according to the Scriptures. —1 Corinthians 15:1–4

MAP LEGEND:

This passage in 1 Corinthians is sometimes referred to as a creed, because in it the Apostle Paul states the basic beliefs of the Christian faith.

QUESTION 7

In 1 Corinthians 15:1–4, the Apostle Paul summarizes the gospel, the good news of Jesus Christ. Keeping this passage in mind, what would you say if someone asked you to explain the basic beliefs of Christianity?

_____

_____

_____

_____

READ: Ephesians 2:8–9, Romans 3:22, Romans 5:21, Philippians 3:9

For it is by grace you have been saved, through faith—and this not from yourselves, it is the gift of God—not by works, so that no one can boast.
—Ephesians 2:8–9

This righteousness from God comes through faith in Jesus Christ to all who believe ... —Romans 3:22

Just as sin reigned in death, so also grace might reign through righteousness to bring eternal life through Jesus Christ our Lord. —Romans 5:21

... Not having a righteousness of my own that comes from the law, but that which is through faith in Christ—the righteousness that comes from God and is by faith. —Philippians 3:9

QUESTION 8

In general, do you think people would rather try to earn their way to heaven or rely on God's grace? Explain your answer. How would you compare God's grace with trying to be good enough to get to heaven (for example, what are the pros and cons of each)?

_____

_____

_____

_____

READ: Ecclesiastes 3:11, 1 John 5:13

He has made everything beautiful in its time. He has also set eternity in the hearts of men; yet they cannot fathom what God has done from beginning to end. —Ecclesiastes 3:11

I write these things to you who believe in the name of the Son of God so that you may know that you have eternal life. —1 John 5:13

QUESTION 9

Have you ever sensed that you are eternal (that you will live for eternity)? Why do you think you felt that way? Was it something you arrived at logically, something you felt in your heart, or a little of both?

_____

_____

_____

_____

QUESTION 10

On a scale of 1–10, how sure are you that you will spend eternity in heaven? Circle your answer below and explain why you chose that number.

1   2   3   4   5   6   7   8   9   10

READ: John 14:6, Acts 4:12

Jesus answered, "I am the way and the truth and the life. No one comes to the Father except through me."—John 14:6

"Salvation is found in no one else, for there is no other name under heaven given to men by which we must be saved."—Acts 4:12

GODQUEST

MAP LEGEND:

In the Acts 4:12 verse, the Apostle Peter is speaking before the Sanhedrin, the Jewish ruling council, and he is referring to Jesus. When Peter finished speaking, the Sanhedrin was astonished by his courage and the miracles the apostles had performed, yet the Jewish rulers threatened Peter and commanded him not to speak again of Jesus.

QUESTION 11

We've now reached the last discussion question in the *GodQuest* study, and it's a good time to summarize what you've learned. What do you believe about how to reach God and an eternity in heaven? What *path* are you taking?

_____

_____

_____

_____

Close your weekly study with prayer. If you're doing the *GodQuest* study in a group, ask group members to share prayer requests; then close your group meeting in prayer.

THIS WEEK, BE SURE TO COMPLETE *THE WEEKLY QUEST* AND THE DAILY *TRAVEL LOGS*.

If you would like to dig deeper into the topics from this week, read Signpost 6 in the *GodQuest* nonfiction book by Sean McDowell and Stan Jantz.

The Weekly Quest

The lists that follow include some of the topics we covered this week, along with suggested books, websites, and resources. Pick one or more topics and do a little research of your own. After you complete this week's *Travel Logs*, you might want to circle back to this section. The *Travel Logs* might arouse your curiosity about a specific topic.

THE BASICS OF CHRISTIANITY

Books:

- *Mere Christianity* by C. S. Lewis
- *Knowing God 101* by Bruce Bickel and Stan Jantz

Websites:

- **AllAboutGod.com.** This website is filled with easy-to-understand material that answers some of the most common questions about God, archaeology, the Bible, and other religions.

THE EVIDENCE FOR CHRISTIANITY

Books:

- *The New Evidence That Demands a Verdict* by Josh McDowell
- *The Case for Christ* and *The Case for Faith* by Lee Strobel
- *More Than a Carpenter* by Josh McDowell and Sean McDowell
- *The Reason for God* by Timothy Keller
- *Is God Just a Human Invention?* by Sean McDowell and Jonathan Morrow

Websites:

(Websites not described here were featured in past Signposts.)

- SeanMcDowell.org

- Josh.org

- LeeStrobel.com

- ConversantLife.com. ConversantLife.com is focused on real-life spiritual conversations. Look for *Belief* or *Believe* under "The Current" or "Columns." You might also want to check out the Q&A pages.

- **Stand to Reason: STR.org.** Stand to Reason has a website packed with articles, podcasts, blogs, a training curriculum, and a store with a variety of resources.

EVALUATING RELIGIONS AND RELIGIOUS BELIEFS

Books:

- *Choosing Your Faith* by Mark Mittelberg

- *Jesus Among Other Gods* by Ravi Zacharias

- *World Religions and Cults 101* by Bruce Bickel and Stan Jantz

- *Five Sacred Crossings* by Craig J. Hazen

Websites:

- **Acts 17 Apologetics Ministries: Acts17.net.** The story and apologetics ministry of Nabeel Qureshi (see the Day 3 *Travel Log*). This site features a number of articles and videos, as well as the full article referenced in the Day 3 *Travel Log*.

DAY 1
Did You Know?

The chart below describes the basic beliefs of five of the most popular religions in the world.

RELIGION	BELIEF ABOUT GOD	THE PATH TO ETERNITY	ATTITUDE TOWARD OTHER RELIGIONS
Buddhism	There is no god	Enlightenment	Other religions are false
Hinduism	There are many gods	Reincarnation	All religions are true
Islam	One god (Allah)	The Five Pillars	Other religions are false
Judaism	One God (Yahweh)	Obeying the law	Other religions are false
Christianity	God the Trinity (Father, Son, and Holy Spirit)	God's grace and faith in Jesus Christ	Other religions are false

A recent study of religious beliefs in America[1] found that:

• 43% of Americans agree with the statement "It doesn't matter what religious faith you follow because they all teach the same lessons."

• 40% of Americans agree with the statement "All people will experience the same outcome after death, regardless of their religious beliefs."

After reviewing the chart of the major religions, what do you think? Indicate your level of agreement with the two statements from the survey:

_____

_____

_____

_____

_____

_____

_____

_____

_____

_____

It doesn't matter what religious faith you follow because they all teach the same lessons.

__ Strongly Agree __ Agree __ Uncertain __ Disagree __ Strongly Disagree

All people will experience the same outcome after death, regardless of their religious beliefs.

__ Strongly Agree __ Agree __ Uncertain __ Disagree __ Strongly Disagree

[1] Barna Research Group, "What Americans Believe About Universalism and Pluralism," http://www.barna.org/faith-spirituality/484-what-americans-believe-about-universalism-and-pluralism; accessed 18 April 2011.

Your Faith Path

(Courtesy of Mark Mittelberg, author of *Choosing Your Faith*, *The Questions Christians Hope No One Will Ask*, and *The Reason Why*.)

Do you know why you believe what you believe about God or about spiritual matters in general? Most people haven't stopped to think about their reasons or about how they arrived at their beliefs—but it's vitally important to do so. Maybe it would help to summarize the ways most of us have selected our beliefs. Here are six approaches or "faith paths" that individuals use to choose their faith:

FAITH PATH	DESCRIPTION	ASSESSMENT
Relativistic	Assuming that whatever they believe magically becomes true for them	Tempting, but it doesn't work in any other area of life, so why trust it in the spiritual realm?
Traditional	Passively accepting the teachings passed down by their parents or teachers	These teachings could be right, but you need to test traditions to make sure they're based on truth.
Authoritarian	Submitting to the ideas of a powerful leader or organization	These ideas could also be correct, but the credentials and message of those authorities need to be weighed carefully.
Intuitive	Relying on spiritual instincts or hunches	Instincts too can sometimes be helpful, but without further information, they can also lead you down blind alleys.
Mystical	Believing what they think God told them directly	God *can* speak to us, but 1 Thessalonians 5:21 cautions us to *test everything … hold on to what is good*, and Galatians 1:8–9 warns against accepting any teachings that contradict the biblical message.

Evidential	Using logic and real-world facts to scrutinize spiritual teachings	We're wise to apply these inescapable God-given tests—logic and evidence—to all truth claims, including any ideas we've picked up through the other faith paths. Jesus often helped His listeners overcome their doubts about His teachings by appealing to His works and miracles. In effect, He was saying, "Not only do my words make sense; my actions provide the evidence that what I'm saying is true!" First Thessalonians 5:21 and the rest of the Bible support this approach.

After reading through this description of the six paths to faith, which one(s) best describes how you've arrived at your beliefs about God?

_____

_____

Do you agree with Mark's assessment of your path (or paths)? Why or why not?

_____

_____

How satisfied are you with the path you've been on? Would it be helpful to choose another path as you move forward in your spiritual journey? If so, which one?

_____

_____

WANT MORE? For more information about the six faith paths, as well as twenty compelling reasons that support the claims of Christianity, see *Choosing Your Faith* by Mark Mittelberg.

GODQUEST PROFILE: NABEEL QURESHI

Nabeel Qureshi was born in California to devout Muslim parents who had immigrated to the U.S. from Pakistan. Nabeel's father was an officer in the U.S. Navy, and the family lived in various locations in the eastern United States as well as in the U.K.

As part of his Muslim upbringing, Nabeel learned Arabic before he was even taught English, and by the age of five, he had not only read the whole Qur'an in Arabic but had even memorized many chapters. He recited part of the Qur'an every morning and religiously went through five daily prayers. Nabeel even learned many evidences for his faith, and he was devoted to the teachings of Islam.

In 2001, Nabeel became friends with David Wood, who was a Christian apologist (defender of the Christian faith) as well as a devoted follower of Jesus. The two men launched into earnest discussions about the evidence for both religions. Nabeel questioned the accuracy of the Bible; David talked about the evidence provided by thousands of manuscripts. Nabeel had been taught that Jesus never claimed to be God; David countered with Scriptures showing Jesus' claims of divinity. Nabeel had read in the Qur'an that Jesus had not died on the cross, but after reviewing historical accounts, he came to realize that Jesus' death had been clearly established.

After investigating Christianity, Nabeel then turned his focus on an intense examination of Islam. While there were many things he loved about the religion, Nabeel was unable to find clear proof that Muhammad was a true prophet of God.

As the years went by and Nabeel searched for the one true God, he was amazed at the miraculous ways God answered his prayers. In the end, it wasn't just the evidence that convinced Nabeel to turn to Christianity, it was the love and grace of a God who would send His own Son to atone for human sin.[2]

[2] Adapted from "Crossing Over: An Intellectual and Spiritual Journey from Islam to Christianity" by Nabeel Qureshi, http://acts17.net/articles/nabeelstestimony.htm

What do you think was the most difficult part of Nabeel's *GodQuest*, and why?

_____

_____

_____

_____

_____

_____

_____

_____

Over time as he searched for God, Nabeel made a decision to follow the
evidence and the truth, wherever it might lead. Take a moment and think
about your own life and your beliefs. Would you be willing to truly search for
God, no matter where that might take you? Explain your answer.

_____

_____

_____

_____

_____

_____

_____

_____

WANT MORE? For more information about Nabeel Qureshi,
visit Acts17.net.

The Path

You broaden the path beneath me, so that my ankles do not turn. —2 Samuel 22:37

You have made known to me the path of life; you will fill me with joy in your presence, with eternal pleasures at your right hand. —Psalm 16:11

My steps have held to your paths; my feet have not slipped. —Psalm 17:5

Show me your ways, O LORD, teach me your paths … —Psalm 25:4

I run in the path of your commands, for you have set my heart free. —Psalm 119:32

Your word is a lamp to my feet and a light for my path. —Psalm 119:105

Trust in the LORD with all your heart and lean not on your own understanding; in all your ways acknowledge him, and he will make your paths straight. —Proverbs 3:5–6

The Bible writers frequently used the word *path* to describe the way we choose to go through life. Which of the verses above do you particularly like? Why?

_____

_____

_____

_____

Look again at Psalm 17:5. Have you ever slipped off the path? What happened, and how did you get back on the right way?

_____

_____

_____

_____

Have you ever taken the wrong path and then had to backtrack? Describe what happened.

_____

_____

_____

_____

_____

Describe the path you're currently following.

_____

_____

_____

_____

_____

How certain are you that your path is the correct one? What could you do to increase your level of confidence?

_____

_____

_____

_____

_____

Reflections from Your Journey

As you think back over the video teaching, discussion questions, and *Travel Logs* from this week, what made the biggest impression on you? Why?

After going through *GodQuest*, what do you believe? Fill in the chart below for each topic or question by stating what you believe and why.

TOPIC OR QUESTION	WHAT DO YOU BELIEVE?	WHY?
Is there a God, and who is He?		
Who is Jesus, and is He God?		
Does heaven exist, and how can you spend eternity there?		
Is the Bible the accurate, authentic Word of God?		

What have you learned during your *GodQuest*? Fill in answers to each of the questions below.

What are the most important things you've learned?

_____

_____

Have your beliefs changed? If so, how?

_____

_____

Has your confidence in your beliefs changed? If so, how? Are you more willing or less willing to discuss your beliefs with other people?

_____

_____

What are the next steps in your ongoing *GodQuest*?

_____

_____

Finish this week's study by spending some time in prayer. Lay before God any doubts and questions you still have. Ask for Him to give you wisdom and teach you through His Word. Talk with God about where you want to go from here and how you want to grow in your faith and build your relationship with Him.

If you don't have a relationship with Jesus Christ, talk with your small group leader about how to invite Jesus into your life. If you are not doing this study with a group, talk with a pastor or a friend you know who follows Jesus.

Next Week: *Your Spiritual Journey Continues on Your Own*

Life is an ongoing adventure when you live in relationship with God, and we hope you continue with the journey of ultimate discovery!

Acknowledgments

From Sean McDowell

My sincere gratitude to the Outreach team for catching the vision for this project. I have been dreaming about doing a project like this for years, and the great people at Outreach made it happen.

Thanks to the school where I teach, Capistrano Valley Christian Schools, for letting me miss a few days for filming. And thanks to my students Sonia, Joseph, and Casey for their feedback on the novel and teen Guidebooks.

Jennifer, I could not have asked for a better coach for this project.

And thanks to my beautiful wife, Stephanie, for encouraging and supporting me throughout this project. I love you!

From Jennifer Dion

With love and appreciation for Alyssa, Jenna, Brandon, and Daniel Dion. May you love God, test all things, and hold firm to your faith for all eternity.

Thank you to my parents, Harold and Sue Aurand, for their lifelong encouragement and for helping transport kids while I worked on this Guidebook.

Sean, thank you for your vision and for all the time and hard work you put into this. You are a pleasure to work with!

From Both

We are very grateful to Barbara Wise, Craig Hazen, Lee Strobel, Josh McDowell, Miles McPherson, Dave Dravecky, Mark Strauss, and Greg Koukl for sharing their time, personal stories, and expertise. *GodQuest* wouldn't have been the same without you! A special thank-you goes to Mark Strauss for helping with the Exodus 3:14 interpretation.

We wish to acknowledge the organizations that provided locations for the *GodQuest* videos: Fallbrook Land Conservancy, Capistrano Valley Christian Schools, Colorado Christian University, Mission San Juan Capistrano, Palomar Pomerado Health, The Rock Church, Bethel Seminary, Biola University, Cherry Hills Community Church, and Stand to Reason.

A big thank-you goes to Matt Jensen, Matt Mangham, and their team at 4120Productions.com. We appreciate your creativity, patience, and flexibility. You definitely earned your M&Ms.

We would like to thank Illustra Media for allowing us to use some of their excellent video footage in the Signpost 2 lesson.

With gratitude to Carol Lusteg, who single-handedly tracked all the details and insured that the *GodQuest* project stayed on schedule.

Thank you to our amazing editors, Toni Ridgaway and Diane Stortz, for making this book the best it could be.

Thank you also to Mark Mittelberg and Stan Jantz for providing excerpts from their books.

Tim Downs and Alexia Wuerdeman did an incredible job with the graphics—thank you!

Finally, we would like to acknowledge Scott Evans, Eric Abel, and Dave Bordon for their input, creativity, and backing for this project.

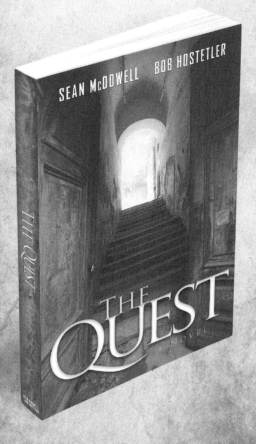

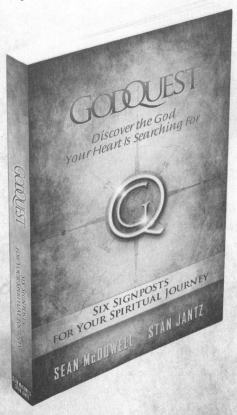